JESUS
The Fact Behind the Faith

JESUS

The Fact Behind the Faith

by

C. Leslie Mitton

William B. Eerdmans
Publishing Company　　　Grand Rapids, Michigan

232.908
M 698s

Library of Congress Cataloging in Publication Data

Mitton, C Leslie.
  Jesus: the fact behind the faith.

  1. Jesus Christ—Historicity.   I. Title.
BT303.2.M57   232.9'08   73-20193
ISBN 0-8028-1563-4

CONTENTS

Preface, 7

1. The Problem, 9

2. The Sources of Our Information, 31

3. The Influence of Faith on History, 41

4. The Importance of the Historical Element
   in the Gospels, 56

5. Evidence of Historicity in the Gospels, 67

6. Criteria for Distinguishing Historical
   from Nonhistorical, 80

7. Historical Features in the Portrait of Jesus, 87

8. Historical Facts in the Ministry of Jesus, 105

9. The Teaching of Jesus, 133

Addendum, 148

Conclusion, 150

Select Bibliography, 152

5

PREFACE

In recent years extreme statements have been made by prominent scholars suggesting that all knowledge of what the historical figure of Jesus was like is in fact totally beyond recovery. They suggest that the early Church imposed its faith in Christ as Lord upon the material in the gospels to such an extent that genuinely historical features, so far as they may exist, are no longer discernible.

This kind of statement has disturbed and unsettled many whose lives are committed to faith in and service of Jesus Christ. This is all the more regrettable because the statements are grossly exaggerated. It is our belief that a vivid, unmistakably historical figure can be discovered within the gospel records. Certainly this figure is presented in a way that embodies something of the faith and devotion of those who wrote the gospels, but it is not distorted beyond recognition. This figure indeed is recognizably the same as the figure of Jesus who meets us in the earliest form of the tradition within the synoptic gospels.

This book does not aim to contribute anything to the scholarly discussion of this important question, but is written for the benefit of ministers and school teachers with special responsibility for Christian education, who themselves have felt the disturbing influence of the extreme skepticism already referred to, and have met questions raised by it among their congregations and senior classes. They wish to know how, if at all, this historical skepticism can be answered. They do not want merely soft answers of reassurance, but an honest investigation and genuine arguments, if they are to recover any confidence that the figure of Jesus that meets us in the gospels is not just a creation of human imagination but basically a real historical person, of whom we can form a clear picture. Such a figure, we believe, does meet us in the gospels. The historical person of Jesus whom we can discern there is that of the very person about whom those who knew him best came to believe the most astounding things—that God had uniquely confronted them in that life, in both the words and deeds of Jesus. It was this historical figure which awakened faith in them, and can still awaken faith in men and women today.

I regret that the splendid book by Professor J. Jeremias on *The Proclamation of Jesus* (Vol. I of his *New Testament Theology*) did not become available till the work on this present book was almost complete. Only occasional references to it have been introduced. It is, however, a most important book for all who are concerned to know all they can about the historical Jesus, and is to be commended most strongly.

Chapter 1

The Problem

On the front cover of the *Spectator* on January 23, 1971, great prominence was given to some words of Professor Trevor Roper, Regius Professor of Modern History in the University of Oxford. They were:

> The plain fact is that we know nothing about the historical Christ. . . . The gospels, after all, tell us a lot of palpable rubbish. . . . The Church created Christ.

The words were taken from his review of Professor C. H. Dodd's book, *The Founder of Christianity*. Professor Roper was sharply dissenting from the less skeptical view adopted by Professor Dodd. Professor Roper's point of view is, however, one that many other scholars share. It is not surprising, therefore, if Christian people who are not scholars find themselves disturbed. Is it really true, they ask, that nothing certain is known about the historical Jesus?

The desire to be sure what in the gospels may be regarded as really historical is not new, though the urgency of the questions about it has in recent years become more desperate. Early in this century the question was put with real hopefulness: "What was the historical Jesus

really like?" Scholars then believed that with the new
critical knowledge of the gospels recently made available
to them, they had the means of distinguishing between
what in the gospels was historical and what was nonhistorical. By this means they believed that they could
reach behind the artificial figure of the divine Christ as
he had been molded by an other-worldly piety and pom-
pous ecclesiastical traditions, and rediscover within the
gospels the real figure of Jesus of Nazareth. More recently, however, this confident search for the historical
Jesus has become very much more tentative, and the
form of the questions much more wistful, even appre-
hensive. The kind of question now being asked is: "What
can be known of the historical Jesus?" or even: "Can we
know anything of the historical Jesus?"

This may seem a very strange state of affairs to one
who is not familiar with the issues being currently, and
vigorously, debated among New Testament scholars. Have
we not four gospels that purport to tell us a great deal
about Jesus of Nazareth? That is, of course, true. But
we are living at a time when every religious belief is
being sharply challenged. Even belief in God is widely
questioned, and even among those who honor Jesus there
are many who would not now treat seriously the Church's
claim that he is the Son of God in a unique sense, but
would regard him only as a very remarkable man. The
Bible also is no longer regarded as a divine book whose
every word is literally true, but a compendium of writings produced by men just as liable to error and ignorance
as other men. It is no longer possible merely to quote
the official teaching of the Church or the words of Scrip-
ture as an answer to the question: "What can we know
about Jesus?" because immediately the further questions
are raised: "How can we know that what the Church or
the Bible teaches is reliable?" "How far can the gospel
records about Jesus be treated as factually accurate, or
to what extent have they been modified and embellished,
perhaps even created, by pious imaginations?"

From time to time the entire story of Jesus in the

gospels has been dismissed as "myth" or "legend" with
little or no historical foundation at all. Sometimes, for
instance, the official Communist line, with its professed
atheism, has been to relegate the whole story of Jesus
to the realm of myth and fiction, or even ascribe it to
the machinations of capitalist propaganda. More recently
Allegro's much publicized book, *The Sacred Mushroom,*
has argued elaborately a new case for regarding the story
of Jesus as a folk myth, something that took shape out
of the mind of man to give expression to his longings,
needs, and fears, but without any foundation at all in
historical fact. No competent scholar, however, has accepted Allegro's theories, which seem to border on the
fantastic.

The most serious questioning in recent times of the
historicity of the story of Jesus in the gospels has come,
in fact, not from anthropologists or atheistic propaganda,
but from the researches of Christian scholars, some of
whom find themselves honestly convinced that the gospels should not be treated as factual records of historical
events but as expressions of Christian faith in pictorial
form. They argue that the people who wrote the gospels
themselves passionately believed that Jesus was the Son
of God, who had been miraculously raised from the dead
and whom they worshiped now in his exalted position
at "the right hand of God." When therefore they wrote
about his human life they could not help but read back
into it something of their own estimate of him. They
wrote not to report facts, but to persuade their readers
to see Jesus as now they saw and understood him. They
superimposed their present faith onto the past records
of his life, thus embellishing them beyond recognition,
perhaps even handing on as factual history episodes and
sayings that might be true of the heavenly Son of God,
but did not in fact actually happen.

It is against this strongly argued point of view that
modern students of the New Testament find themselves
facing the old question in a new and highly skeptical
form: "What can we really know about Jesus?" Is there

in the gospels historical fact that we can be sure of? Are
there words attributed to him that we can believe he
really spoke? Or is it true, as some contend, that in the
gospels we have only a pictorial representation of what
the early Church came to believe about Jesus? Some, like
Professor Roper, abandon hope of recovering actual historical information about Jesus. Others, still hoping, ask:
"Is there not some way of penetrating behind what came
to be believed by the early Church to that which actually
happened?" For many people this has become an exceedingly important question, and much seems to them
to depend on the answer that must be given to it.

The History of the Inquiry About the Historical Jesus

In the 1920s in Great Britain the overriding concern
among New Testament scholars and theological students
was the search for "The Jesus of History." It was then
confidently believed that the critical tools for the study
of the Bible had now been developed that would enable
them to discard the embellishments in the gospels and
penetrate to the real historical figure behind the theological figment that the intervening centuries had con-
structed around him. One book seemed to symbolize this
widespread concern. It was T. R. Glover's famous vol-
ume *The Jesus of History*. But there were other books
representing the same point of view and emphasis, for
instance, J. A. Findlay's *Jesus as They Saw Him* and
H. D. A. Major's book about Mark's gospel, significantly
called *Jesus by an Eyewitness*. In this wave of confidence
many writers produced biographical studies of Jesus—
some of a scholarly nature, some more popular in their
appeal.

It was an exciting time in which to be a student, and
those who were involved in it remember this approach
to the gospels not just as an intellectual exercise but as
an interest that brought great enrichment to their faith

as Christians. We believed then that through the pages of the gospels, especially the first three, if we approached them with the discernment that recent critical study had made possible, we could begin to see with considerable clarity the actual human figure of Jesus, which we felt had over the centuries become sadly obscured and distorted by much of traditional and conventional piety. The creeds spoke of him in remote and abstract language as "Very God of Very God" and "of one substance with the Father." Classical art portrayed him predominantly as Man of Sorrows, Lamb of God, Judge at the right hand of God. In stained-glass windows all too often he was made to appear effeminate and unnatural. All of these, we felt, were far removed from the strong, prophetic, dynamic character that we glimpse within the gospel story in his contacts with both friends and opponents.

It seemed to us then to be tremendously important to discover as accurately as we could what the real Jesus was like, since his was the human life in which and through which God had taken such significant action. We felt there was good reason to believe that this real historical figure was discernible within the gospel narratives, even if it was superficially blurred and obscured by later additions and distortions. It was a figure strikingly at variance with the portrait that conventional piety had produced, a figure characterized by courage and manliness as well as gentleness, by inflexible determination as well as an utter lack of self-concern, by gaiety and humor as well as scrupulous honesty and sincerity. We tried—no doubt in this case with misguided enthusiasm—to find traces in the records that gave hints of his characteristic gestures, and the way bystanders recalled the effect of his voice and eyes. It seemed at that time that the real Jesus of Nazareth was being set free from a sacred icon within which the Church and theology had confined him for centuries. A false and misleading representation of him that had long prevailed unchallenged was at last being destroyed. Jesus was being enabled to become himself again, rescued from the distortions of art and piety.

He was stepping out again into the very midst of life,
where his ministry had been exercised and where indeed
he truly belonged. Günther Bornkamm, in *What Can We
Know About Jesus?* (p. 72), writes of the excitement and
thrill that this movement brought to those who shared
in it: "The popularity of this movement, which has probably not been equalled by any other in theology, was indeed only too understandable. For here, it appeared, the
history of the Lord and his personality were finally made
visible and life-like, freed from dogmatic petrifaction, removed from the sphere of theological metaphysics and
set immediately into the present."

In Germany this search for the historical Jesus was
often associated with an attitude of skepticism toward
Christian orthodoxy, with an expectation that Jesus once
discovered would be reduced to the stature of an ordinary human being. In Great Britain, however, this was
not the case. Those who gave themselves most enthusi-
astically to this study acknowledged Jesus as Lord and
Saviour in whom God had uniquely approached the world
of men. They wanted to know more about Jesus as he
actually had been in order to know more accurately what
that human life was like in which God had so fully revealed himself and so significantly taken action. Indeed,
the study, so far from leading students to skepticism,
often proved a most valuable aid in their devotional life.
In private prayer people were encouraged to relive in
imagination the actual scenes from the gospels in which
Jesus had been present, confident that in this way they
were very close to God himself in his dealings with men.

The Critical Evaluation of the Gospel Materials

This "Jesus of History" research at the beginning of
this century had been made possible as a result of the
new critical approach to the gospels that had been established in the preceding decades. This, it was claimed,

had provided the means of distinguishing, to some degree at any rate, between the authentic and the inauthentic, between what actually had happened and what later narrators and editors had read back into the story.

This new critical approach had reached certain conclusions, which were then largely regarded as firmly established and reliable. They may be summarized as follows:

(1) John's gospel was placed in a category quite separate from the other three, which were described as "synoptic." It was recognized that the fourth evangelist had not made it his aim to portray the plain historical facts about Jesus. In his gospel we were not presented with the real human figure of Jesus, but rather a semi-divine person moving majestically on his way to the cross. In this book, therefore, it was clear that the developed Christian faith of a later time had been read back into the story. It was theology more than history; it offered primarily interpretation of the eternal significance of Christ, and was interested in historical fact only as it could be made the means of disclosing Jesus as Son of God with superhuman powers.

The traditional belief that it was John the son of Zebedee, an eyewitness of the ministry of Jesus, who had written the gospel had been discarded and the date of the gospel was placed at the very end of the first century or even later.

In the search for historical facts, therefore, the fourth gospel could be almost entirely dispensed with. The fact that it had been written so long after the events it records made more credible the claim that in it faith and interpretation had been superimposed upon historical fact.

(2) It had also been established that Mark's gospel was unquestionably the earliest of the four, and that Matthew and Luke had both borrowed extensively from its material. Mark, therefore, was the nearest to the actual events that his gospel reports, and so, almost certainly, was the one least likely to be seriously affected by later modifications.

This conclusion was something quite new and of immense importance. The age-old tradition of the Church had taught that Matthew was the earliest of the gospels, written by an actual disciple, and so full of firsthand information. It had, of course, long been recognized that Matthew and Mark shared a very great deal of the same material, often presented in almost identical language. The traditional explanation of this interdependence had been that Mark's gospel was an abbreviation of Matthew's, though it was extremely difficult to suggest any credible reason why Mark should do such a pointless thing. Certainly in the history of the Church until quite recent times Matthew's gospel had stood out as the predominant one, with Mark's gospel almost unnoticed in the background. This is not surprising, since if Mark was in fact merely an abbreviation of Matthew, it was a peculiarly unimportant document that hardly deserved to survive.

It had also long been recognized that Luke had large areas of material that he shared either with Matthew alone or Matthew and Mark together. Again the accepted solution had been that Luke had borrowed extensively from Matthew.

The new critical studies had, however, completely revolutionized this traditional understanding of the relationship between the first three gospels. It was now proved beyond doubt that Mark was the earliest of the gospels, and that both Matthew and Luke, quite independently of each other, had borrowed extensively from Mark. This gave Mark a most impressive status of historical reliability. Not only did it make him the earliest of the three, and therefore the one nearest to the events described, but the fact that both Matthew and Luke had independently used his work so fully clearly showed that they both regarded it as a document of quite special reliability.

This demonstration of the earliness and importance of Mark brought to the forefront an old tradition in the Church that had long been ignored, and indeed seemed a most improbable story if, as had been believed, Mat-

thew had been the earliest gospel and Mark only a peculiarly inept curtailment of it. This tradition, which could
be traced back to a very early date, reported that Mark
had derived his material from Peter, and indeed the New
Testament itself testified to a close relationship between
the two men (e.g., I Peter 5:13). Now that Mark had
been proved to be the earliest of the gospels this old tradition assumed a new probability. It could be shown that
some of the narratives in Mark did sound as if they came
from an eyewitness. They contained lots of little details,
insignificant in themselves, but just the kind an eyewitness
might well recall. So the link of Mark with Peter was
accepted as a serious possibility, and this gave greatly
added weight to the probability of its historical reliability.
Indeed, it was on the basis of this assumed relationship
between Mark and Peter that Major wrote his little book
on Mark, already referred to, and called it *Jesus by an
Eyewitness*.

(3) Other material also was discovered in Matthew and
Luke that clearly came from a date much earlier than
either of them. Apart from the passages that both Matthew
and Luke derived from Mark, there are also considerable
sections, consisting largely of the teaching material of Jesus,
which Matthew and Luke have in common, and which
for the most part are almost identical in wording. Since it
was no longer thought possible that Luke had known
Matthew's gospel and borrowed directly from it, some other
explanation was necessary. The one that seemed best
able to account for these sections of almost verbal identity
in the two gospels was that there were written records
of the teaching of Jesus in existence before the time of
Matthew and Luke, to which each of them independently
had access and from which each borrowed extensively.
These early records came to be known, for convenience,
as "Q." The close similarity of wording in these sections
in Matthew and Luke, and the fact that the sayings were
often associated with each other in the same order in
both gospels led to the conclusion that these early rec-

ords must have been known to Matthew and Luke in a *written* form, and not just orally.

Since Q existed early enough for both Matthew and Luke to use it independently and presumably in different parts of the ancient world, it was felt that an early date must be accorded to this material as well as to Mark. A date around A.D. 65 was suggested for each of them; some thought an even earlier date was probable for Q.

(4) It was also argued that the material peculiar to Luke was also of an early date, and therefore historically reliable. Some believed that there was good reason to think that Luke had in fact combined this material with the teaching material borrowed from Q into a single document before he came to know about Mark. They saw reason to believe that the material he took from Mark was inserted into this document as a kind of afterthought. If this were so, then Luke's special material (usually for convenience called "L") was also very early—as early perhaps as Mark, and if so probably of considerable reliability.

In contrast scholars came to regard the narrative material in Matthew, which is peculiar to that gospel, as very late, and for this, and other reasons also, historically suspect.

The early date of Mark, Q, and L was therefore regarded as established beyond reasonable doubt on the basis of impartial critical methods, and by virtue of their earliness they were believed to preserve a large amount of historical material. These three early sources seemed to stand out as reliable in a way that other sources were not. Items that were found in them had every right to be regarded as basically historical and worthy of a high degree of confidence. They were believed to be relatively free from doctrinal and legendary distortions. They had come into existence within a generation of the death of Jesus. They had been written while there were many eyewitnesses of the ministry of Jesus still living. The apostle Paul, as he gives his list of the eyewitnesses of the resurrection appearance of Jesus in I Corinthians 15, makes special reference (in v. 6) to the fact that most of these witnesses are still alive, and therefore able to confirm his statements. Mark, Q, and L may be regarded as coming from a date not much later than Paul's letters and so at a time when eyewitnesses were still living who could confirm or deny what was written in them.

New Testament scholars, therefore, in the 1920s generally believed that what was preserved in these three primary sources, which could be isolated within the synoptic gospels, provided material that historically was of a very high order. It was relatively free from modifications imposed by developing doctrine or ecclesiastical discipline, because these influences had not yet become dominant. This, however, did not mean that everything in these sources was automatically accepted without question. It was recognized that even within the space of a single generation natural human tendencies would affect the reporting. A tendency to exaggerate would make itself felt almost at once, and there would be an understandable tendency to adapt a saying to make it fit more pointedly the circumstances of the reporter and his readers. The miraculous elements also would be heightened in the telling. In consequence it was customary to accept rational explanations of miraculous happenings, especially for those miracles classed as "nature miracles," such as the feeding of the multitude, the withering of the fig tree, and the destruction of the herd of swine. If, however, a watchful eye was kept on these recognized tendencies and their effects eliminated, what remained, it was believed, provided materials of a very high degree of historical validity. By means of a discreet use of these materials it was felt to be possible to reconstruct a reasonably accurate portrait of the Jesus of history.

The Reaction

This confidence that scholars had gained a sure access

to the Jesus of history lasted on the continent of Europe till the first world war, and right up to the end of the 1920s in Great Britain. One mark of this confidence was the very large number of Lives of Jesus that were produced, some sober and closely related to the available evidence, such as Goguel's *Life of Jesus,* others much more flamboyant and imaginative, in which the author's own ideas extravagantly elaborated such factual evidence as was to be found within the gospel narratives.

It was, however, a confidence that was to meet a sudden end in a catastrophic change of climate in the realm of biblical and theological studies. The collapse of Europe in 1918 may have had much to do with this change, though its effect was not felt in Great Britain until ten years or so later. Certain personalities embodied this change of mood. They may indeed have helped to produce it, or they may rather have become the mouthpieces of a widespread feeling of disillusionment, which included disillusionment with the earlier theological outlook. Whatever may be the cause of the change, it is clear that a complete reversal of interest swept over the theological field. The leaders of the Jesus of History School, recently admired and applauded, suddenly found themselves not only outmoded and deserted, but even the objects of ridicule. They had believed themselves to be pioneers of a great liberal revival of thought, part of which was to set Jesus free from the shackles of ecclesiastical and theological orthodoxy. To be a liberal in theology and biblical studies had been regarded as praiseworthy. Now suddenly to be a liberal was to be the object of scorn. A new way of thinking, later to be called neo-orthodoxy, utterly usurped its place. The Jesus of History inquiry, which had been one of the great concerns of liberal scholars, collapsed like a pack of cards, along with everything else associated with theological liberalism. Any individuals who retained any loyalty to the discredited movement led a kind of underground existence, hardly daring to admit their interest. With such intolerant impatience can a change of theological climate make itself felt.

The books and authors and new trends that are associated with this dramatic change of interest may be briefly noted as follows:

(1) Albert Schweitzer is best known to the general public today because of his devoted life of Christian service in a missionary hospital in Lamborene, in Africa. Before that, however, he had won fame in several spheres, one of which was that of biblical scholarship. In 1906 he wrote a book that was later translated from the German into English with the title, *The Quest of the Historical Jesus*. This English translation appeared in 1910, but it was not until the 1920s that its full effect began to be felt. At first, under the dominance of liberal theology, it was treated largely as a curious oddity. But its effect, like that of a delayed-action bomb, proved to be of explosive and devastating power. In it Schweitzer reviewed every Life of Jesus that had been written between 1750 and 1900. With consummate skill he demonstrated how curiously different they were from each other, and how differently Jesus was interpreted in them. Each author seemed able to manipulate the evidence in the gospels so as to fashion a figure of Jesus after his own heart. Subjective preference seemed able to mold the material into any shape it wished. The effect of the book on its readers was to leave the impression that it was totally impossible for anyone to produce an objective characterization of Jesus. The material available was not of the kind that made impartial history possible. The central figure of Jesus belonged so much to his own time that a biographer inevitably distorted him beyond recognition as he tried to present him as a person who could be intelligible to readers of his own time and nationality. We inadvertently seem always to reproduce him in the image of our own cultural environment or our own subjective aspirations.

Schweitzer particularly denounced the inadequacy of the liberal picture of Jesus, and accused its authors of deliberately closing their eyes to real features of the gospels that they personally found distasteful, for instance, the apocalyptic elements that were unmistakably present.

It must be conceded that Lives of Jesus had not been objective and impartial. For some curious reason, when men write about Jesus they seem to assume that in him should be embodied all their own deepest convictions and highest ideals, and all too often they force these ideals back upon Jesus, instead of allowing what they find in him to shape and control their own ideals and standards.

(2) Another figure, whose influence exceeded and outlasted that of Schweitzer, was Karl Barth. In 1918 he wrote his defiant commentary on the Epistle to the Romans, though it was not until 1932 that it appeared in an English translation. He saw liberalism in theology, with its confident attempt to use human skills and reasoning as the means by which man could understand God, as totally, even wickedly, wrong. The only knowledge of God that man may have, he declared, is that which comes from God by revelation. What he found in Paul's Epistle to the Romans provided confirmation and authorization for this emphasis. In the postwar years of disillusionment people seemed ready to listen to this message that hope must be placed in something other than mankind, and Barth became the dominant figure in the sphere of theology for more than a generation. Indeed, it became the fashionable thing to be a Barthian, and to be known as a liberal was to be relegated to a theological backwater, indeed to be almost a traitor to the essence of the Christian faith.

The old liberalism was therefore swept aside, and all that went with it, including the deep interest in the human figure of Jesus. The new center of interest was the Word of God. This eternal Word was what God had spoken in the Bible; man can only listen to it, and be convicted and convinced by it. There was no way from man to God, not even by way of historical research into the person and work of Jesus of Nazareth. Barth even wrote: "So far as we can get back to the historical Jesus, there is nothing remarkable to be found in his life and character and teaching." Great man as Barth was, this saying can only be assessed as monstrously untrue. The human figure of Jesus had proved itself to many involved in the Jesus of History research as utterly wonderful, commanding, and soul-searching. Barth also said: "In history as such there is nothing as far as eye can see to provide a basis for faith." It is true, of course, that the historical Jesus does not automatically awaken faith in everyone. Some who encountered him personally in his ministry saw only one who was "a gluttonous man and a winebibber." There were others, however, who came to acknowledge him as the Son of God. It is God and God alone who awakens this insight, said Barth. The historical figure does not of itself create faith. That is clearly true. But surely it is also demonstrably true that both in the time of Jesus and in the Jesus of History research that historical figure could and did prove the means by which God awakened faith.

Barth helped to condition men's ears, at least the ears of the theologically minded, to hear God's voice, particularly in the New Testament's offer of justification by faith alone, and in the Gospel as presented in Pauline categories. And this emphasis was one of the factors in turning men's eyes from the historical figure of Jesus of Nazareth and minimizing its importance.

(3) Another factor that tended in the same direction was the discovery of the so-called "kerygma," and especially the claim that this, rather than the historical Jesus, should be regarded as the starting place for the proclamation of the Gospel. Dodd's small but very important book *The Apostolic Preaching* (published in 1936) gave for the English reader a clear outline of what is meant by the kerygma. A preoccupation with the kerygma proved to be more congenial to Barth's theological emphasis than concern with the Jesus of history had been, though in fairness it should be said that Dodd himself never set the two in contrast to each other.

Kerygma is the word used for the first proclamation of the Christian Gospel as the earliest missionaries carried it out into the world. What did it consist of?

Had a representative liberal of the Jesus of History school been asked this question, he would probably have given some such answer as this: "The earliest message was surely the story of the life of Jesus, his teaching and his healing ministry, his death and resurrection, proclaimed as God's offering of himself to man. It included a special emphasis on the Fatherhood of God with its complement, the brotherhood of man." To men of that time this had seemed obviously true, and it had not been noticed that the epistles of the New Testament and the Acts of the Apostles give little or no support to it.

If we consult the New Testament itself to find out what this earliest form of Christian proclamation was, we find it consisted of something like this: "God promised through his prophets of old that he would in due time take action and set his people free from their distresses and humiliations. This promise God has now fulfilled in Jesus, who lived a life of practical goodness and yet was put to death by wicked men on a cross. But he conquered death by rising from the dead, and has been received at God's right hand. He now sends to his people the gift of the Holy Spirit, and in God's own time he will come to judge all mankind and to claim the world for God. Therefore men should repent now and come to terms with God without delay, while there is still time."

This is the outline of the kerygma which the apostles are recorded as preaching in the early chapters of Acts, and the substance of it, in whole or in part, can be found repeated at various points in Paul's letters, especially perhaps in sections where he seems to be quoting the agreed message of the Church rather than merely stating his personal convictions.

The theme of the kerygma was, therefore, what God had done in Christ for mankind. It was not at all in the first place a careful recounting of the facts of the earthly life and teaching of Jesus. The real Christ was in fact the living Christ who reigned at God's right hand, the transcendent Christ, rather than the human figure whom the liberal theologians had so zealously tried to reconstruct.

It was pointed out that there was very little about the human life of Jesus in the epistles of the New Testament, and that Paul's Gospel can be presented with scarcely more than a passing reference to it. Is it right, therefore, it was asked, to represent an accurate knowledge of the human Jesus as so extremely important?

In consequence, by many scholars the kerygma came to be treated as the fundamental core of the Christian faith, and the story of the human life of Jesus was relegated to a subordinate position, certainly not essential, perhaps even not very important for true faith.

(4) For students of the New Testament there was still another factor, a factor even more decisive than the three already named, in turning men's thoughts from the Jesus of history and creating an atmosphere in which any search in that direction came to be regarded as both unnecessary and futile. This was the development of what in English became known as Form Criticism of the gospels, although in fact it was only one branch of the Form Critical School, the radical branch associated with the name of Rudolf Bultmann, which was to prove another source of skepticism about the historicity of the gospels.

Source criticism of the gospels had by this time explored almost every avenue open to it, and achieved considerable results. The careful study of the gospels to determine their relation to each other, and to isolate the sources on which each depended, had led to the general recognition of the priority of Mark, the use by Matthew and Luke of Mark and also of Q, and the existence of two other "sources" in the material used by Luke alone and by Matthew alone (L and M). But this research into literary antecedents could not be traced back beyond the years A.D. 60-65, and this was thirty years after the death of Jesus.

A new interest began to absorb scholars' attention. It began to be asked what we might find out about the way this tradition about Jesus had been passed on during this period of thirty years, when it was preserved only in human memories and communicated by word of mouth, before anything about it was written down. The question to be answered was: In what form or forms was the tradition transmitted? The inquiry came to be known as *Formgeschichte* in Germany, the land of its birth, and Form Criticism in English-speaking countries. Such "forms" were found in the miracle and healing stories, in some recognizable patterns in the teaching material, particularly the method of the parable, and in what came to be known as "Pronouncement Stories." These are stories in which the narrative is reduced to a minimum and used merely as an explanatory introduction to an important pronouncement by Jesus. There are many examples of this form in the gospels. Instances of it may be seen at Mark 2:15-17, 18-19, and 23-27.

At first this seemed an interesting study with no particular bearing on the matter of historicity. Indeed, one of its leading exponents, Dibelius, argued that it helped to establish historicity, particularly in the case of the Pronouncement Stories. These, he argued, were already established and settled in their particular "form" when Mark availed himself of them. Therefore they must take us back to a period considerably earlier than Mark's gospel.

In the hands of Bultmann, however, Form Criticism became a tool that was to be used to discredit the gospels as historical documents. He argued that all the material in the gospels had existed during the oral period, not as connected sequences or continuous narratives, but as small individual units. These were remembered and used, not out of historical interest, but because the unit, whether narrative or teaching material, served some useful purpose in the early Christian community. If it could be used to suggest an answer to some problem in the life of the Church, whether intellectual, moral, or practical, then it was preserved, and its practical usefulness led to its preservation. What the three synoptic evangelists had to work with, therefore, was a large assortment of small independent units, entirely cut off from their original context in the ministry of Jesus, and remembered only because they met some need in the post-resurrection Christian communities. All the evangelists had to do when they compiled their gospels was to string these disconnected items together into a connected story.

This new approach in itself did not discredit the historical element in the gospels. Bultmann, however, used these premises to draw some disturbing conclusions that did have this effect. He argued:

(a) Mark's function as the earliest of the evangelists had been merely to string together as best he could, but without any knowledge whatever of their original chronological sequences or of their context in the ministry of Jesus, the many separate units he found available in the life of the Church in the area where he lived. His supposed link with Peter was dismissed as pious legend, the only purpose of which had been to provide authority for the gospel. The claim that eyewitness evidence was to be found in Mark was discounted as foolish credulity. Mark's gospel was simply a collection of items that some section of the early Church had used for its own guidance and edification. The other gospels, being later than Mark, were even further removed from historicity.

(b) Bultmann also argued that during the oral period, as the individual items were told and retold in order to meet some pressing need of the early Church, they would be continually subjected to changes and modifications. They would be adapted little by little from what they had been at first to something more directly applicable to the needs of the Church. Some modifications can, in fact, be detected, but many others, he argued, took place, even though no evidence of the adaptations can any longer be found.

(c) Even more than this, Bultmann ascribed to the early Christian communities astonishing powers of creation. He argued that under what was claimed to be the immediate guidance of the Holy Spirit, early Christian prophets declared what they believed to be some direct message from the risen Christ, and this saying in the course of transmission came to be ascribed to the earthly ministry of Jesus. Many sayings and incidents, he claimed, came not from the ministry of Jesus at all, but sprang out of the life of the later Christian community. They may be described as "community sayings" or "community creations."

This has led Bultmann to insist that what we have in the gospels is not at all factual history, but the faith of the early Church. They reflect the faith of Christians during the period that followed the death and resurrection of Jesus. They are therefore firsthand evidence for what was believed among Christians of this period; but the materials in them have been so molded and modified by this later faith that they cannot be said to preserve reliable, historical materials at all. Our earliest starting point historically is therefore the kerygma of the early Church, the message that the Church in the early days heard and proclaimed. This we find reflected in the gospels. But to step back from that, over a period of more than thirty highly formative years, to the facts of history is no longer possible. Bultmann's devastating conclusion has often been quoted:

> We can no longer know the character of Jesus, his life, or his personality. . . . There is not one of his words which we can regard as purely authentic. We can sum up what we can know of the life and personality of Jesus as "simply nothing."

These four influences all played some part in producing a situation in New Testament scholarship in which people freely said that no Life of Jesus could ever again be written, that the historical Jesus was forever totally irrecoverable, and that the ground of our faith was not the historical person of Jesus, but the eternal Christ as proclaimed in the kerygma.

We hope to try to show later that Bultmann's extreme skepticism about the historical materials in the gospels is quite unwarranted. Possibly he himself used the method

of exaggeration to arouse people to thought. Certainly in
later books he has been willing to allow that there are
some few items in the gospels that may be regarded as
factual and authentic. But the extreme skepticism of his
approach, made all the more compelling by his dominating position in the world of scholarship, has come to be
largely shared by a whole generation of New Testament
scholars. It is this which makes the background of our
present inquiry. Bultmann asserts that we cannot know
anything reliable about the historical figure of Jesus. This
claim, however, seems to us a great exaggeration.

Bultmann is an extremely great man who has exercised a dominating influence on younger scholars, especially those who know him personally. He gathered around
him a group of these very able men who adopted his
point of view and became exponents of it. Many of
these have since then become eminent scholars in their
own right, making their own important contributions to
New Testament studies. Some of them, however, have
found themselves compelled by their further researches
to diverge from Bultmann's extreme position of historical
skepticism, and have made their own constructive contributions toward a new approach to the discovery of the
historical element in the gospels, what is sometimes called
"The New Quest of the Historical Jesus."

Many people have felt that Bultmann's attitude to the
historical element in the gospels is entirely destructive,
mounting a serious threat to the Christian faith as a whole.
In fairness to Bultmann it must be said that he himself
does not see it at all in this way. He believes that he is
helping the Church to place its faith where faith ought
to be placed, in God and his eternal Word to man, and
not on some ambiguous piece of historical investigation.
He fears that some may elevate an imagined knowledge
of the historical Jesus into a substitute for the total commitment of faith to the living Christ. His books that interpret the Christian message as expounded by Paul and
John reveal a deep and penetrating understanding of
the Christian Gospel, for which the reader is immensely

grateful. But his aggressive skepticism about the historical element in the gospel record seems to be far in excess of what the evidence requires. We may well have to acknowledge that the materials available to us do not enable us to draw up a chronological account of the life of Jesus, or describe his personal appearance. But behind the gospel records there is a clearly discernible portrayal of a real person with strongly marked individual characteristics. We cannot deny that legendary accretions have been added and that doctrinal influences have led to modifications, but these do not totally obscure a recognizably real figure.

Bultmann says that it is impossible any longer to obtain accurate knowledge of the historical Jesus. He also regards it as *undesirable*, lest such knowledge should become what has been called "a secular substitute" for real faith. But if this was a real danger, the grim reality of the incarnation itself would hardly seem to have been either necessary or desirable. A beautiful myth about a divine figure who came to earth and died and rose again would have served just as well. But most Christians feel instinctively that if the record of the life of Jesus is treated as nothing more than edifying fiction, no matter how full it may be of spiritual significance, something absolutely essential has been lost.

We therefore proceed on the assumption that it is most desirable to gain as clear a picture as the evidence allows of the figure of Jesus of Nazareth as the people of his own time saw him, because we believe that it is in this historical figure more than at any other point in human history that God has made himself known to men and acted for the good of men. We believe, moreover, that from the evidence in the gospels it is possible to recover a reasonably accurate understanding of what this historical figure of Jesus was like.

Chapter 2

The Sources of Our Information

Clearly the gospels provide the fullest accounts of Jesus of Nazareth that have come down to us, though some items of information about him are found in other parts of the New Testament as well. Are there, however, sources of information apart from the New Testament?

The answer is: "Very little indeed." But we had better look briefly at such as there is. From the point of view of the Roman Empire the life and death of Jesus was an unimportant episode that took place in a remote and obscure corner of its vast territory. It is not surprising that their historians did not specifically record it. They were interested in extension of territory and struggles for the imperial succession. But though references to Jesus are missing, there are references to the early Christian movement. Pliny, a Roman governor in Asia Minor, wrote to the Emperor Trajan in the year A.D. 110, asking for guidance concerning his treatment of Christians in his province, but the information he gives deals with the practices of the Christians, not with their founder. Suetonius similarly refers to the Christians and the disturbances in which they were involved. He also makes precise mention of their founder as one called "Chrestos." Tacitus also comments, in connection with the burning of Rome at the time of Nero, that the Christians, who were being blamed for the fire, owe their origin to "Christ, who was condemned to death during the reign of Tiberius by the procurator Pontius Pilate." This comment affords an interesting confirmation of some of the information provided by the gospels.

Josephus was a Jew of the first century A.D. who wrote a history of the Jewish people. There are references to Christ in this work, but some of them at any rate are thought to be insertions by Christians introduced into the text at a later time. As such they are of no independent value. There is one comment, however, that has every likelihood of being genuine. It refers to the death by stoning of someone called James, who is described as "the brother of Jesus who was called the Christ."

These secular historians may be said to confirm that Jesus actually lived, and was executed under Pontius Pilate, and that his followers continued as a vigorous and defiant group that went on growing long after his death. It is not in itself very much, but it is enough to counter the extreme claim of some skeptics that Jesus in fact never existed at all, but is only a myth or a folk legend.

Another possible source of information is the apocryphal gospels. During the second century there were in existence many writings known as "gospels," in addition to the four that finally were accepted into the canon of the New Testament. Those which were excluded from the official canon of the Church came to be known as "apocryphal." Some of them had enjoyed considerable popularity before they were finally rejected. Among the better known of these were the gospel of Peter, the gospel according to the Hebrews, the gospel according to the Egyptians, the gospels of Philip and Thomas. These have been in the main lost and are known only through quotations from them that have been preserved in other writings that have survived.

Compared with our four canonical gospels these are fan-

tastic and even ridiculous. One is deeply grateful for
the wisdom of the Church that excluded them from the
New Testament, even though some of them claimed to
be written by one of the twelve disciples. By comparison
the three synoptic gospels are impressive for their so-
briety, moderation, and good sense. These qualities are
in striking contrast to the sometimes gross and even offensive improbabilities of the apocryphal gospels. Indeed,
to many people this marked contrast with the synoptic
gospels seems a very strong argument in favor of the
general reliability of the synoptic record.

In the 1950s there was great excitement over the discovery of the Dead Sea Scrolls and other evidences of a
nonconformist Jewish colony living a kind of monastic
life in a settlement at Qumran on the Judean shore of
the Dead Sea. The scrolls, which were found hidden away
in jars in inaccessible caves high up in the steep cliffs of
the area, had originally belonged to the library of this
community, which is usually thought to have been connected with the strict and ascetic group known as the
Essenes. The scrolls that have been found consist mainly
of copies of books of the Old Testament in their original
Hebrew. Other books, in Aramaic, described the rules of
the community. It is clear from these books that the members of the community were very critical of official Judaism
and especially of those who were in charge of the temple
and its services. The leader of the community, a greatly
revered figure, is spoken of in the scrolls as "the teacher
of righteousness."

As often happens with new discoveries, there were at
first greatly exaggerated accounts of the importance of
these documents for the Christian faith. It was claimed
that as a result of the discoveries our concept of early
Christianity would be entirely revolutionized. Some even
identified Jesus with the teacher of righteousness, and
argued for a close link between the community and the
original disciples of Jesus. This, however, has all proved
to be merely irresponsible speculation. Further studies
have failed to establish any direct link at all between

the community at Qumran and the work of Jesus. The nearest link that sober scholars have dared to suggest, and they agree that it is only a possibility for which there is no direct evidence, is that John the Baptist may have had some association with it. No significant light, however, is shed by the scrolls on the historicity of Jesus, though they have provided valuable insights into the state of Judaism at the time of Jesus and an increased knowledge of the form of Aramaic probably spoken by Jesus himself.

Another interesting discovery of old documents took place at Nag Hammadi some ten years later. These documents have not all been published yet, but they appear to have been writings treasured by a Christian community in Egypt that was far from orthodox. It seems to have been a sect of Gnostic Christians, who finally separated from the main body of the Church. Among these writings are two that were already known by name. They are the gospel of Thomas and the gospel of Truth. Neither is what we normally think of as a gospel. The gospel of Thomas is a collection of sayings ascribed to Jesus but without any narrative. Some of the sayings are similar to words of Jesus recorded in the four gospels. Others that have no parallels in the canonical gospels are often quite fantastic and immediately recognizable as inauthentic. Professor Jeremias has made a strong case for regarding one or two of the sayings, not already known to us through the canonical gospels, as genuine, but not all scholars are able to concur in this. It cannot be said, therefore, that this "gospel" adds anything to our knowledge of Jesus.

Still less historical material comes from the gospel of Truth. This is a kind of semi-philosophical dissertation, having no connection with the Jesus of history. Indeed, the unorthodox Christians at Nag Hammadi, if they were, as is supposed, of a Gnostic type, were the kind of Christians who did not take seriously the humanity of Jesus. They tended to argue that it was only an "appearance" and not a reality at all. So these two "gospels" have helped us no more than the apocryphal gospels in our quest for historical information.

How far do the other books in the New Testament, apart from the gospels, give us useful information? The answer is: "Not very much." But there are some valuable items, indeed more than many are inclined to allow. We will look first at Paul's letters.

It is sometimes claimed that Paul attached no importance whatever to the human life of Jesus, that Christ was for him the living Christ, the Saviour and Lord and Judge of men, far more than he was an historical figure of the past, and that the living Christ totally overshadowed the human Jesus, even to the point of excluding him from Paul's thought.

It is, however, quite false to say that Paul's letters reveal no knowledge of the earthly life and ministry of Jesus. In fact, from the incidental references in them one can build up a fairly adequate picture of the human Jesus, and one that tallies with that of the gospels.

Concerning the facts about Jesus' life and death we gain from Paul the following pieces of information: Jesus was a man; he was a Jew; he was descended both from Abraham and from King David; his earthly life was lived in poverty; he had brothers, one of whom was called James; he fulfilled his ministry among the Jews; he had a band of twelve disciples; very careful details are given about the last supper Jesus took with his disciples and about the words he spoke on that occasion; he was betrayed to his enemies; he died at the time of the Jewish Passover; he was put to death by crucifixion; this implies that the Roman authorities carried out the execution; but his death was contrived by the Jewish leaders; he was buried; he was raised on the third day afterwards; he appeared to many witnesses who are most carefully listed in order and some of them named.

There are also aspects of the character of Jesus that are mentioned by Paul. He speaks of the meekness and gentleness of Christ, his obedience to his Father's will, and his steadfast endurance. He speaks of himself as an "imitator of Christ," which suggests that he had a fairly clear picture of the kind of person Jesus was. Some, perhaps here venturing into the area of speculation, have pointed out that Paul used, apparently interchangeably, two such phrases as "Put on Christ" and "Put on love" (*agape*) and suggested that this implies that for Paul Christ and *agape* were identifiable, that *agape* summed up what he knew of Jesus, and that this is what he meant when he spoke of imitating Christ. It was the same as "making love your aim," as he says elsewhere. If this were so, then the great hymn in I Corinthians 13 expounding the qualities of *agape* may have been written out of the awareness of what he knew about Jesus.

There are some sayings of Jesus recorded in Paul's writings. There is the one that forbids a Christian man to divorce his wife, one that authorizes proper financial support for those who give up remunerative work in order to serve the Christian community full time, and also those words spoken at the Last Supper which have been regarded as the words of institution of the sacrament of the Lord's Supper. In much of the ethical teaching of Paul there are continual echoes of the kind of teaching to be found on the lips of Jesus in the Sermon on the Mount, for instance, words about loving enemies and non-retaliation and love being the "fulfilment" of the Law.

It is important to notice that where Paul has a precise word of Jesus, which he can quote in relation to a matter under discussion, for him it is final. There is no place for argument after that. In comparison, his own considered judgment, even though he believes it is prompted by the Spirit of God, is subject to the possibility of human error, and is contrasted with the complete and conclusive authority of a word known to come from Jesus (I Cor. 7:10; cf. I Cor. 7:12 and 40).

There is a saying of Jesus, not recorded in the gospels, that Paul is represented as quoting in some words attributed to him in Acts 20:35: "It is more blessed to give than to receive." It is perhaps not without significance that Luke at any rate regarded it as quite in character that Paul should support his argument by reference to words that Jesus was known to have spoken.

Another New Testament epistle, which traditionally was ascribed to Paul though clearly not from his hand, the Epistle to the Hebrews, makes even more direct reference than Paul to what is remembered of the human life of Jesus. The human life of Jesus meant a great deal to this writer. From this letter we learn that Jesus was tempted (2:18; 4:15); that he prayed with cries and tears (5:7)— perhaps a reference to Gethsemane; he proved himself obedient to God even through suffering (12:2-3); he was gentle to the erring (5:2). He was also a preacher of salvation (2:3), followed by disciples who repeated his message (2:3).

This letter not only appeals to facts and features of the human life of Jesus, but also specifically insists on the full reality of the incarnation. This is a matter of great importance to the writer. He says that Jesus was a partaker of flesh and blood (2:14); his life on earth is referred to as "the days of his flesh" (5:7). He shows a preference for the human word "Jesus" over more exalted titles (e.g., 2:9; 12:2; 13:12, etc.).

I Peter makes frequent references to the sufferings of Jesus and also to the fact that he was "rejected" (2:4) and "reviled" (2:23). He died on a "tree" (2:24; 3:18) in spite of his innocence of any crime (3:18), and met all his humiliations in a spirit of nonretaliation (2:23).

The Epistle of James tells us nothing about the earthly life of Jesus, but there is no book among the epistles of the New Testament that is so obviously aware of the teaching of Jesus, especially that type of teaching which is included in the Sermon on the Mount. Nor is there any other that reflects so sensitive an understanding of the teaching, even though he may not precisely quote the actual words of Jesus.

It is, therefore, a great distortion of the facts to suggest that Paul and the authors of the other New Testament epistles show no interest in or knowledge of the historical figure of Jesus. A considerable body of information about him can be built up from them.

We must concede, however, that our knowledge of the human life of Jesus would be exceedingly fragmentary if we had nothing to turn to except the epistles. It is in the gospels that the fullest information is to be found, and especially in the three synoptic gospels. The fourth gospel, however, has its own contribution to make, even in providing purely factual data. Fifty years ago, during the Jesus of History period, it was customary to rule out the fourth gospel entirely as a possible source of historical information. It was treated as entirely a spiritual interpretation of the significance of Jesus, which quite deliberately read back the living Christ into the figure of Jesus. Where some apparent fact was stated, it was assumed that its purpose was to convey some symbolic meaning, and it might very well have been invented for this purpose.

It was also believed in that period that the fourth gospel had been written much later than the other three, and therefore the author must have been familiar with them. Where the narrative, therefore, coincided with that of the synoptics, it was regarded as borrowing from them, and so adding nothing to what was already known. Where it differed from them, it was said that the fourth evangelist was deliberately altering them but only to serve some subtle theological purpose—not at all because he had any superior historical knowledge. So far as any historical reconstruction of the ministry of Jesus was concerned, the fourth gospel was entirely ignored.

In the intervening years, however, the attitude of scholars to the fourth gospel has undergone a striking change. More and more of them are becoming convinced that the fourth evangelist did not in fact know the other three, but wrote his gospel in total ignorance of them. This is a remarkable development, because it means that where the fourth evangelist confirms facts and sayings in the synoptic gospels, he is not merely repeating their evidence, but is in fact giving an independent witness. If the Christian tradition reached the fourth evangelist by an entirely different route from that of the synoptics, it means that within the fourth gospel there is available to us a further independent witness to the events in the story of Jesus. In 1963 C. H. Dodd wrote a long and comprehensive study, *The Historical Tradition in the Fourth Gospel.* In it he argues convincingly that some material from that gospel can be used to supplement, perhaps even correct, as well as confirm what comes to us from the synoptic tradition.

The gospels, therefore, especially the three synoptics, but not wholly to the exclusion of the fourth gospel, are the primary source of historical knowledge about Jesus. Even these, however, it must be conceded, were not primarily written as history, though Luke 1:1-4 makes it quite clear that this writer at any rate had historical accuracy as one of his main purposes. Their basic aim, however, is not merely to provide an impartial statement of objective facts. They unashamedly present the story of Jesus from the point of view of those who believed him to be the Son of God and the source of man's eternal salvation, and who wished others to come to this same conviction. They are clearly intended as propaganda, not as disinterested chronicles. It is a mistake, however, to think of propaganda as necessarily false. If a man seeks an appointment with a business firm it may be because he greatly admires its products and has reason to believe that there are no others in the world so good. His own use of its products has proved it. In that case his commendation of its goods is supported by his honest belief in its truthfulness. So the early Christians passed on what they believed about Jesus as unsurpassed good news, but they believed that it was actual truth, which did not need to be exaggerated and improved upon. As with every first-class commodity, the truthful description of it is the best form of advertisement.

It has to be acknowledged, however, that in the gospels, even the most historical of them, the author's faith is being presented as well as merely historical records. The evangelist is trying to help us to make a right assessment of Jesus, as well as know some facts about him. It is, as Nineham wrote in his Pelican commentary on Mark, written largely from the same point of view as Bultmann's: "The gospels give us, inextricably fused together in a single picture, the historic Jesus and the Church's understanding of him, as it developed over half a century or so" (p. 51). Sometimes Nineham gives the impression that in his judgment "history" cannot in fact be distinguished from interpretation and that to make the attempt is entirely futile. At other times his words strike a more hopeful note, as when he writes (p. 50): "The Jesus of Mark is beyond doubt basically a figure of early first century Palestine and not an invention of first century Rome" (where Mark's gospel is usually believed to have been written).

So we take courage and make it our aim to find means of isolating later interpretation in the gospels from historical reporting, and to discover what the historical picture of Jesus is like, when nonhistorical features have been eliminated. Then we can see if this in the main confirms or contradicts the overall impression left on us as we read the gospels in their present form.

Chapter 3

The Influence of Faith on History

One of the chief causes of doubt about the historicity of the figure of Jesus as presented in the gospels is the argument that the materials out of which the gospels were produced were for a whole generation used orally in the teaching and preaching of the Church before being written down. Those who passed on these oral traditions were people who believed in Jesus as their Lord, the Son of God, one who had risen from the dead, and in their use of them they hoped to persuade others to accept the same faith in Jesus that they held. Inevitably, therefore, the original facts of history would come to be embellished and heightened by the faith of the narrators, in order that the narratives would more readily serve the purpose of those who told them.

This must undoubtedly have happened to some extent, though not necessarily to the extreme degree visualized by Bultmann. Any attempt to distinguish the historical from the nonhistorical in the gospels must therefore allow for this effect of faith upon the telling of history.

It is, in fact, a feature that New Testament scholars have had to allow for over all the years of this century, and not just since the emergence of Form Criticism. The scholars who worked within the earlier Jesus of History researches were well aware of it. They too learned to allow for embellishments, and it was part of their aim to detect and eliminate them. They recognized them particularly and most easily in the modifications introduced by Matthew and Luke into the material they took over from Mark. Both these later evangelists made changes with the purpose of accommodating what Mark had written to a point of view more acceptable to themselves and to their readers of a generation later than Mark. Indeed, it was one of the strong arguments in favor of the priority of Mark that where Matthew and Luke differed from Mark in their wording they reflected theological and ecclesiastical interests characteristic of a later period. These modifications in Matthew and Luke of Markan material are so well known that it will be sufficient to indicate just one or two of them briefly:

(1) Matthew and Luke tend to remove or modify Mark's somewhat blunt and careless sentences about Jesus, and they do this apparently in the interests of the developing faith of the Church with its exaltation of the person of Jesus:

(a) At Mark 6:5-6 Jesus is described as receiving a very cool reception at his home town of Nazareth. Mark concludes the episode with the comment: "He could do no mighty work there, except that he laid his hands on a few sick folk and healed them. And he marvelled because of their unbelief" (RSV).

At Matthew 13:58 this becomes: "He did not do many mighty works there, because of their unbelief." Matthew discreetly omits Mark's reference to the fact that Jesus "could not" do any mighty works, since this suggests an undignified restriction of the power of Jesus. He also omits the words about Jesus' surprise, since this also implies a limitation in Jesus' knowledge.

By the time Matthew wrote, reverence for the divine nature of Jesus made it appear inappropriate that he should be represented as limited either in power or knowl-

edge. Faith here, then, is seen adjusting a factual statement in Mark. No doubt it was not intended to distort
the truth, but merely to correct what now appeared as
a regrettable infelicity in Mark's wording, which, Matthew
honestly believed, misrepresented the truth about Jesus.

(b) At Mark 10:18 a man ran up to Jesus and knelt
before him, and addressed him as "Good Master." Jesus
takes him up on this and replies: "Why do you call me
good? No one is good but God alone." Matthew changes
the form of the man's question to: "Teacher, what good
deed must I do to have eternal life?", so that the reply
of Jesus can also be changed to: "Why do you ask me
about the good? One there is who is good. . . ." Clearly
Mark's version is original and Matthew has made a very
awkward alteration in order to avoid the suggestion in
Mark's version that Jesus objected to being called "good,"
and, by adding that no one except God is truly good,
seemed to imply that he himself was not worthy of the
description. Matthew, no doubt reflecting the growing
sense in the Church of the perfect goodness of Jesus,
felt that Mark's wording must be altered to avoid an
implied disparagement of him.

(c) In Mark 4:38 the disciples are very frightened as
their boat runs into a fierce storm. They are agitated and
resentful that Jesus is quietly sleeping through it all. They
arouse him with the petulant question: "Teacher, do you
not care if we perish?" His indifference to the danger
suggests to them a lack of proper concern for his friends'
safety. The words also show the disciples in an unfavorable
light—as frightened, agitated, disrespectful to their master,
and sadly unaware of his power to deal with the situation.

Matthew changes this to: "Save, Lord, we are perish-
ing" (8:25). The disciples' petulance has been eliminated
and the power of Jesus is acknowledged by implication.

Luke also (at 8:24) feels the need to modify Mark's
wording and he gives: "Master, we perish," which also removes the offensive elements.

(2) It is also noticeable how Matthew and Luke tend
to modify the harsh references in Mark to the disciples.

For Matthew and Luke these men were now reverenced as Christ's apostles and as such entitled to the utmost respect. Instances of the determination of these evangelists to protect the reputation of these honored figures of the past by altering Mark's plain-spoken comments include the following:

(a) After the stilling of the storm (Mark 4:40) Mark represents Jesus as saying to the disciples: "Why are you such cowards? Have you no faith even now?" (NEB). Matthew omits the words altogether and Luke is content with the less disparaging question: "Where is your faith?" (Luke 8:25).

(b) At Mark 9:6, as he tells the story of the Transfiguration, Mark makes no attempt to disguise the terror in Peter's heart and the foolishness of the question he asks in his agitation. He comments sardonically: "He did not know what to say; they were so terrified."

Matthew at 17:4 omits the sentence altogether and Luke softens it to: "He spoke without knowing what he was saying."

(c) At Mark 10:35 James and John privately asked Jesus for the privilege of sitting on his right and left in the coming Kingdom. We do not wonder that the other ten "were indignant" when they heard about this attempt by the two brothers to corner special advantages for themselves.

Matthew, however, exonerates them by making their mother, prompted by ambition for her sons, make the offending request.

These three items illustrate how the later faith of the Church introduced changes into the earlier tradition at the expense of historical accuracy. Many other similar instances can be quoted.

(3) Similarly, we find the later evangelists amplifying the words used by Mark about Jesus in the interests of ascribing greater glory to him as Christ:

(a) At Mark 8:29 Peter's confession of Christ at Caesarea Philippi is in the words: "You are the Messiah" (NEB).

At Matthew 16:16 the reply has been extended to: "You are the Messiah, the Son of the living God."

(b) In Mark 1:10, at the baptism of Jesus, what happened is described as an inward experience of which no one but Jesus was aware: "Jesus . . . saw the heavens opened. . . . A voice said: *Thou* art my beloved Son."

In Matthew 3:16 the personal experience has been turned into an objective miracle which others who were present were aware of. The heavens *were opened* (not that Jesus experienced them as opening). A voice said: "*This* is my beloved Son." It is represented that the voice addressed the people, not Jesus.

(c) At Mark 13:14 Jesus is made to refer vaguely to some coming disaster that will overwhelm Jerusalem: "When you see 'the abomination of desolation' usurping a place which is not his" (NEB).

Matthew makes this much more specific and in line with what actually happened in A.D. 70: "When you see the abomination of desolation standing in the holy place [i.e., the temple]. . . ." Luke alters it differently, but also in line with what he knew, by the time he wrote, had actually happened: "When you see Jerusalem encircled by armies. . . ."

Matthew and Luke have modified the words of Jesus in Mark, to make them correspond more exactly with actual events. Mark's recorded words are much more likely to represent what Jesus actually said than the modified form of the words in Matthew and Luke. Their more detailed forecasting of events, put back on the lips of Jesus, would increase the readers' reverence for him in view of the very accurate foreknowledge of future happenings here ascribed to him.

(4) The influence of later times upon the form of the early tradition can also be seen in the way some of the severe elements in the moral teaching of Jesus were softened by Matthew to bring them more within the reach of church members at a time when the words of Jesus were coming to be regarded as fixed rules to be enforced by discipline.

(a) Both Mark and Luke report that Jesus spoke words insisting that in God's intention a husband should never divorce his wife (Mark 10:11; Luke 16:18). In both cases where Matthew reports this teaching he introduces the well-known exceptive clause, which was interpreted to mean that in the case of a wife's adultery a husband was entitled to claim the right of divorce (Matt. 19:9; 5:32).

(b) The same kind of tendency can be discerned if one compares later manuscripts of the gospels with earlier ones. The genuine reading at Matthew 5:22 has: "Every one who is angry with his brother shall be liable to judgment." But in the later manuscripts, from which the Authorized Version was translated, this exacting standard has been modified into something much less rigorous: "Whoever is angry with his brother *without a cause* shall be in danger of the judgment." We are certainly nearer to what Jesus actually spoke in the earlier version.

(c) Even within Mark itself, though here there is no objective basis of comparison, an apparent contradiction within the text seems sometimes to lead one to suspect that the later Church is being allowed to register its point of view as different from that of Jesus himself. At Mark 2:19 Jesus speaks as though fasting is something quite inappropriate among his followers: "Can the wedding guests fast while the bridegroom is with them?" he asks, implying that his presence is like that of a bridegroom in the marriage celebrations and that fasting is incompatible with the joy of the occasion.

It is known, however, that the early Church resumed the Jewish practice of fasting after some time, having in some areas at any rate fairly rigid rules enforcing it.

A good case can therefore be made out by those who think that the following verse in Mark is the Church's later attempt to explain why their own practice is at variance with the words of Jesus: "The days will come, when the bridegroom is taken away from them, and then they will fast in that day" (Mark 2:20). Certainly verse 19 has a higher claim to historicity than verse 20, though the suspected alteration is one that cannot be demonstrated with the same confidence as those based on an objective discrepancy between a later document (such as Matthew) and an earlier one that it is reproducing (such as Mark).

Even before the days of Form Criticism the Jesus of History School used these palpable differences between documents and inconsistencies within the same document to establish what in the gospels is likely to be historical and what should be assigned to the editorial work of the later Church. It was possible by these methods of comparison to recognize the kind of changes that later writers were inclined to introduce, changes that reflect the theological and ecclesiastical point of view of the later writer. The Form Critics, however, were not interested in the changes that can be noted by a comparison of documents. Their concern was with the pre-documentary tradition. Bultmann would claim that the kind of changes that we can actually see taking place in Matthew's treatment of Mark had in fact been going on during the whole period of the oral tradition. Mark himself, and even his predecessors, were just as guilty of it as Matthew, but we cannot detect the changes as readily because the form of the earlier tradition is not known to us. It is claimed that changes were being made all the time as the tradition was transmitted in order to accommodate the traditional material to the developing point of view and changing needs of the later Christian communities. This argument may well be true, but when there is no other document on which a comparison can be based, the assessment of what is original and what is later adaptation becomes very much a matter of subjective judgment, a matter of opinion rather than fact.

We ourselves argued that Mark 2:20 was probably a reflection of the later Church's approval of fasting, whereas Mark 2:19 with its apparent discouragement of fasting had a good claim to be historical. Arguments can sustain this position, but when all is said it remains a more subjective judgment than one based on a comparison between an earlier and a later document. For instance, a comparison between Mark 8:29 and Matthew 16:16 shows objectively that "Son of the living God" occurs in Matthew but not in Mark; therefore on the assumption that Matthew is later than Mark and used Mark, these words are of later origin than the words recorded in the Markan version of the incident.

Most of the judgments of the Form Critics have to depend, however, on subjective opinion. They state what seems to them to be later and nonhistorical, but in many cases there is no objective basis for their opinion. Bultmann, for instance, would classify the whole incident of Peter's confession at Caesarea Philippi and also the Transfiguration as nonhistorical. They are for him devices that the later Church invented in order to give expression to beliefs about Jesus that they had come to hold. But this is opinion, not demonstrated fact, and other scholars feel justified on the same evidence in believing that behind both incidents is a solid core of historicity, even if the stories may have changed a little in the telling. Similarly, the account of the Temptations of Jesus in Matthew 4:1-10 and Luke 4:1-12 are confidently relegated by Bultmann to the status of a "theological construction" produced by the later Church to explain its understanding of the matter. The other possible explanation that Jesus himself at a later stage in his ministry gave his disciples this pictorial description of tensions that tormented him in the early days of his ministry is dismissed without serious consideration. But the dismissal is based on a considered opinion, not on a demonstration of fact.

It must be conceded, therefore, that later writers did alter the tradition as they received it, to make it express more clearly the faith as they had come to hold it and understand it. Where two documents related to each other can be compared, this process can be objectively recognized. But where there is no basis of comparison, we should continually remind ourselves that any judgment expressed is not based on objective evidence, but is largely a subjective assessment, and in all subjective judgments the presuppositions of the assessor inevitably play a large part.

Bultmann, however, contends not only that the tradition was greatly altered in the course of its transmission, but that some incidents concerning Jesus and sayings attributed to him were not so much modifications of earlier material but outright inventions within the life of the early Church—"community creations" as they are called—by means of which the Church expressed and commended its faith.

At first this may seem a very extravagant claim, but again it cannot be denied that it did happen occasionally, even if not as commonly as is sometimes suggested. What makes one hesitate to believe that the early Church frequently invented new material and casually attributed it to Jesus is that the apostle Paul makes it very clear that he himself scrupulously avoids anything of the kind. In I Corinthians 7:10 he quotes the ruling of Jesus about divorce and marriage—"a wife must not separate herself from her husband"—noting that this ruling is not his own, but the Lord's, and therefore authoritative beyond any disputing. In verse 12, however, regarding a marriage where one of the partners has become a Christian and the other remains a pagan, he gives the advice he feels to be best but insists: "I say this as my own word, not as the Lord's." Again in verse 40 concerning the remarriage of Christian widows he gives his own opinion, but adds: "That is my opinion, and I believe that I have the Spirit of God." It is clear therefore that Paul, even when he believed that his advice was given him by the Spirit of God, made a sharp distinction between his own inspired thought and what he had received as a historical word of Jesus.

This should make us hesitate about too readily explaining an episode or saying in the gospels as an invention of the Church, irresponsibly foisted back upon Jesus himself. Paul at any rate took the utmost pains to see that this did not happen.

Yet we must concede that it may have happened and

probably did happen occasionally. The writer of the book of Revelation probably belonged to that class of gifted people in the early Church who are referred to in Paul's letters as "prophets." At least he speaks of what he wrote as "the words of this prophecy" (Rev. 1:3). He, as probably other prophets also, may well have become so vividly conscious of what he believed to be the will of God in some contemporary situation that, like the prophets of the Old Testament, he felt justified in saying: "Thus saith the Lord. . . ." In Revelation 1:8, for instance, he writes: " 'I am the Alpha and the Omega,' says the Lord God." At 1:17 one like a son of man addresses him: "I am the first and the last, and the living one; I died and behold I am alive for evermore, and I have the keys of Death and Hades"—presumably words of Christ, as John was privileged to hear them. Even more precisely at Revelation 22:16 he reports this message which was given to him: "I Jesus . . . am the root and offspring of David, the bright and morning star." It is quite possible that some of these prophetic utterances, giving the words of the living Christ as spoken from heaven, could have been quoted and requoted in the community until in the process they came to be misunderstood as words of the historical Jesus. This *could* have happened, and perhaps we see it happening in the fourth gospel. But it is not without significance that the many words in the book of Revelation of this type (or words of a similar type) do not in fact find their way into the synoptic gospels, attributed to the historical Jesus.

The writer of the fourth gospel is the one who seems to come nearest to adopting this device, but it is almost certain that he used it quite consciously, deliberately ascribing to the historical Jesus what he knew were in fact words of the eternal Christ. It was his conscious aim to let the eternal Christ speak through the figure of Jesus in his gospel. It is most unlikely that the historical Jesus ever said: "Before Abraham was, I am" (John 8:58). That is more likely to be a later theological affirmation of what the Church came to speak of as the pre-existence of Christ.

Even the better-known "I" sayings in John may come into this category: "I am the Way, the Truth and the Life," "I am the Resurrection and the Life," etc. If one were enumerating the words of Jesus with the highest degree of historical probability in them, he would not feel able to include these.

We are, however, on quite different ground when we are dealing with the synoptic gospels, and it is much less likely that we can ascribe the quite different types of sayings found here to the inventive genius of the early Church. It may, of course, have happened sometimes even here. Some moderate scholars have felt that the memorable words of Jesus: "Come unto me, all ye that labor and are heavy laden, . . ." cannot be treated as a historical utterance, but are rather a creation of the Christian community on the basis of the words in Jeremiah 6:16: "Ye shall find rest unto your souls." Others, however, feel that they can without incredulity ascribe these words to Jesus —or at any rate the nucleus out of which the saying developed. Among other things the use of the word "yoke" sounds more characteristic of Jesus than of what we know of the early Church.

Again the striking phrase about the Son of Man being ready to "give his life a ransom for many" has been ascribed to the theological thinking of the later Church. Others again feel that a very strong case can be made for its authenticity.

Some Christians find themselves seriously impoverished when a word they have long treasured as a genuinely historical word of Jesus is described as no more than an affirmation of some early Christian community. It should be said, however, that though this changes our attitude to it, it does not strip the saying of all spiritual value. If it contains a valuable spiritual insight, that insight is still there, even if some early Christian first spoke about it rather than Jesus himself. It means that such a saying would now have the status of an inspired word of the apostle Paul, or John, or the book of Revelation, though not of Jesus himself. For instance, the words placed on the lips of Jesus in the fourth gospel, such as "I am the Way, the Truth and the Life" may not be historically the words of Jesus of Nazareth, but were first used to express what some community within the early Church had come to believe about Jesus Christ, and were valued by the fourth evangelist as embodying a most important truth. The truth in them has the authority of the fourth evangelist rather than Jesus. Supposing instead of placing them on the lips of Jesus in his gospel he had, perhaps in one of his letters, expressed the same truth as his own insight: "Jesus Christ is the Way, the Truth and the Life," it would have been one of the great words of the New Testament because of the insight it contains, even though it would have been a statement about Jesus rather than one by him. Some would claim indeed that its value would in fact be in no way diminished.

One of Paul's many valuable insights was his affirmation that "God was in Christ reconciling the world unto himself. . . ." It is possible to imagine that a similar statement might have been made by an early Christian prophet as a message that the living Christ had spoken to him. In the tradition it might have then come to be referred back to the historical Jesus as if he had said: "In me God is reconciling the world to himself." No essential change in its value as spiritual truth would have taken place. It would still be true whatever the source from which it came.

For critical research, therefore, to remove a word from the category of the words of Jesus and place it among the insights of the early Church does not necessarily deprive it of value. It will, however, make a difference to the way we conceive what the Jesus of history was like. To separate historical words from nonhistorical words later ascribed to Jesus will enable us to gain a clearer picture of Jesus as he was as distinct from the picture that men at a later stage came to have of him.

It is possible also that some incidents, as well as sayings, in the gospels had their origin in the community life of the early Church. Take, for instance, the story of Peter walking on the water. This is one that even cautious scholars would find it hard to ascribe to factual history. It occurs only in Matthew, and belongs to his special narrative source, M, which is regarded as a late source and, on other grounds, the least reliable (historically) of all the synoptic sources. This, along with the difficulty of believing that Jesus would work a miracle of this particular type, inclines even moderate scholars to allow that this must have come into being as the tradition was passed on. How would such a story first be told and later come to be treated as "true"? We do not know. Any answer is largely guesswork. We know that apocryphal stories about Jesus, some of them wildly improbable and fantastic, did begin to be current at the end of the first century. Many of them found their way into the apocryphal gospels, though happily they were in the main excluded from the canonical gospels. The story of Peter, as well as Jesus, being enabled to do the impossible and walk on water was one of these, we may suppose. But how did it win sufficient acceptability to gain a place in Matthew's gospel?

This suggested explanation may be entirely fanciful. We offer it for what it is worth. Let us suppose a company of Christian believers gathered for fellowship. They are always eager to hear any visitor who has any stories about Jesus to tell, especially any that are new to them. One visitor tells this story which he has heard about Peter and how Jesus enabled him to walk to safety over water, at any rate for so long as he kept his eyes firmly fixed on Jesus and kept moving step by step nearer to him. It was only when he allowed his attention to be diverted from Jesus to the threatening elements around and beneath him that he began to sink—until Jesus lifted him to safety. There may have been those present who heard the story with misgiving, doubting whether it did in fact happen like that. Then perhaps there was one in the company who said: "This story is true, because it happened just like that to me." He would then tell his own experience, how when fearful troubles beset him and threatened to over-

whelm him, he found himself enabled to rise above them
so long as he kept his eyes fixed on his Lord and at each
step tried to move nearer to him. It was only when he
allowed himself to become utterly obsessed with his own
fears and doubts that he found himself on the point of
being submerged by them. Even then Christ had come
near to him and raised him up again. This, of course, is
the language of Christian experiénce, not of historical fact.
But one can well imagine that a story about Jesus that
symbolized a spiritual truth about the believer's relation
to the risen Christ would the more readily be accepted
as having a basis in history. The spiritual truth embodied
in this story is much the same as that expressed in Hebrews
12:1: "We must throw off every encumbrance which all
too readily distracts" and "run with resolution the race
for which we are entered, our eyes fixed on Jesus" (NEB
margin). But truth "embodied in a tale" has many advantages over abstract truth.

It is probable also that the story, recorded first in
Mark 15:38, about the rending of the "veil" of the temple
at the time of the crucifixion had its origin in the symbolism it provided for an important and continuing truth
about Christ, the truth that through Jesus and his death
Christians found that the age-old barriers created by
racial differences had been broken down. In Ephesians
2:14 we read: "Jews and Gentiles, he has made the two
one and in his own body of flesh and blood has broken
down the enmity which stood like a dividing wall between." The "veil" of the temple, the curtain that hid
the Holy of Holies from general view, was the symbol
of the exclusively Jewish privilege of drawing near to
God. Those who were not Jews were cut off by it from
God and from God's people. The story of the demolition
of this dividing wall at the time of the death of Jesus
symbolically represented the eternal truth that in his death
Jesus had opened the Kingdom of Heaven to *all* believers,
not just those of Jewish race.·

Items such as these are not to be regarded as historical.
They do not contribute anything to our knowledge of the

historical Jesus. They perhaps came first into being as vivid metaphors which were later transformed into narratives. Their value is that they help to embody and preserve a spiritual truth, and the fact that people find the spiritual truth expressed in a narrative leads them the more readily to accept the validity of the narrative. As Bornkamm put it (in *What Can We Know About Jesus?*, p. 76): "The gospel writers made use of legendary motifs and features in order to make more visible the significance of Jesus as the divine bringer of salvation."

It is part of our task to devise tests by which these legendary accretions can be distinguished from what has a claim to be regarded as historical, not because the legends are totally valueless, but in order that the authentic figure of Jesus may stand out the more clearly, by being separated from inauthentic additions that distort the picture of him.

Chapter 4

The Importance of the
Historical Element in the Gospels

Those who have followed the very radical lead of Bultmann are inclined to insist that it is now impossible for us to reconstruct an accurate picture of the human Jesus. The sources at our disposal do not provide the kind of information that is needed. They are also inclined to add that the recovery of this picture is not even desirable. With it men might begin to substitute a little factual knowledge of the past for the total commitment of faith to God as he comes to us in the living Christ.

The human Jesus, however, as men have found him through the gospels, is one who awakens faith rather than one who provides an escape from it. It is, of course, obviously true that this human figure does not automatically compel faith. As we saw earlier, it made some people sneer: "A gluttonous man and a winebibber," and others shout: "Away with him!" It can, however, bring others to the cry of faith: "My Lord and my God." A knowledge of the historical Jesus does not compel faith, but there is little evidence either that it leads men away from faith. The nearer we can get to a clear picture of Jesus as he was, the more likely we are to be brought to a point of decision about him, as the men of his time were. It may bring many to reject the God who offers himself to us in this figure of history; it may also for many prove the stimulus that creates faith.

Besides the claim that it is impossible and undesirable to be able to find our way to the historical Jesus, there are those who add the word "unnecessary." They argue that the overall picture of Jesus in the gospels, whether historically accurate or not, is all we need. If through that picture the truth about God is mediated to us, that is all that matters. It is not historical knowledge that is important but knowledge of the truth about God, and this can be mediated to us equally by myth and legend as by fact.

This has been the attitude usually adopted by Hindus who are sympathetic to the Christian faith. They argue that truth about God is truth, however it is conveyed. So one Hindu writes: "If the truths which Jesus exemplified and taught are true, then they are true always and everywhere whether a person called Jesus ever lived or not." A contemporary American writer, A. Harvey, represents this point of view from a non-Hindu starting point. He argues that "the power of the Christian message is mediated through 'the image of Jesus' (that is the overall picture of him derived from the gospels).... He is the key image in a parable that the Christian uses to interpret the total reality of which he must make sense.... Jesus becomes a symbol of 'timeless truth'."[1]

There is of course truth in this. What has enlightened and uplifted and saved men down the ages is not the power to discern between factual history and legend in the gospels, but the total figure of Christ as present in the whole of the New Testament, epistles as well as gospels, John as well as the synoptics. But that faith in Christ would have been robbed of much of its nerve and vigor had

---

[1] From "Symbol, Event and Once-for-Allness" (from an excerpt cited by McArthur in In Search of the Historical Jesus, pp. 213-215).

men not felt sure that Jesus had lived and spoken and
acted and died in a way not dissimilar from that recorded
in the gospels. If the whole thing had been shown to be
an edifying fiction with no real basis in fact, much of its
power would have ebbed out of it.

What we need is not to be able to sift history from
legend at every point in the gospel narrative, but the
assurance that the figure we see portrayed in the gospels,
though not identical at every point with the historical Jesus,
is at any rate basically similar to it. If it is all just a
winsomely beautiful story unrelated to fact, many would
feel that their faith had been resting on a deception. We
find ourselves, however, totally able to agree with Althaus
when he writes: "The living eyes of a man look at us out
of the gospels and compel our faith."[2] A real man and
the memory of him lie behind the narrative in the gospels.
If the gospels have embellished the picture a little un-
naturally at some points, we believe that the chief characteristics of this "real man" are still discernible. It is
these we want to reach.

We suggest four reasons why knowledge of the historical
Jesus is important:

(1) The early Church felt it to be important.

Those who argue that knowledge of the historical Jesus
is beyond our reach and that in any case it is not of
the essence of our Christian faith, usually support their
argument by the claim that the early Church was not
particularly interested in the historical life of Jesus, and
that its faith did not at all depend on knowledge of it.
They contend that the early Christians were so preoccupied
with the proclamation of the kerygma, their awareness
of the living Christ, and their belief that he was ruling
at God's right hand and was soon to come again to
earth in judgment and triumph that the past hardly concerned them at all.

If by "the early Church" is meant the Christian community between the time of the death of Jesus and the

---

[2] *The So-Called Kerygma and the Historical Jesus,* p. 45.

writing of the first gospels, then we must insist that we
have very little ascertainable knowledge of what this
Church was like and what it believed. As Downing pointed
out in his book *The Church and Jesus,* scholars tend to
argue in circles. They reconstruct the early Church from the
items in the gospels, which they think came from the
early Church, and then remove these items from the
factual records of the gospels because, they argue, they
reflect the thinking of the early Church. Our only immediate knowledge of the early Church in this period is
that which comes to us from the letters of Paul. Even
here we cannot confidently feel ourselves in direct contact with the *whole* of the early Church. It is not possible
to determine what in the epistles was local to the particular church to which he wrote, or what is representative
of the apostle's own thinking rather than characteristic
of the early Church as a whole. We do not know enough
of this early Church to argue that it lacked interest in
the historical life of Jesus. Such information as we have
does not, however, confirm this dogmatic claim.

The very fact that Mark's gospel was written about
A.D. 65 proves that there was a felt need for information
about the ministry of Jesus. It may be true that the present and the future filled the thoughts of the early Christians far more than the past, but it is also quite clear
that very soon indeed questions about the past began to
be asked with pressing urgency. The question "What
kind of man was this Jesus, in whom God acted so significantly?" must have been one that was often heard.
Otherwise there would have been no need for the materials contained in the gospels. The splendid affirmation
of Philippians 2:6-11 would have been sufficient, supple-
mented by such other kerygmatic material as is found in
I Corinthians 15:1-7 and Romans 1:1-2. The very existence
of the gospels proves that the early Christians did not
find these theological affirmations alone completely adequate. They appear to have asked: "How did it all begin?"
"What kind of things did Jesus do and say?" In particular
another question appears to have demanded an urgent

answer: "How did he come to die?" It is generally believed
that the passion story was the first piece of consecutive
writing to appear. Even before Mark's gospel in its present form came to be written, it is likely there was already
a passion narrative, or, to put it another way, Mark's first
writing may have been the passion narrative. Once, however, this was written, it had to be extended further and
further backwards, to cover first the circumstances of
the arrest and trial, as well as the death itself, and then the
causes of the earlier hostility against Jesus that eventually
led to his death on the cross.

Early Christian writers tell us that at first written records about Jesus were far less attractive to Christians
of that time than the living words of one who had actually
known something at first hand of the ministry of Jesus.
Such an informant, however, would not be welcomed
merely because he could announce the kerygma. One does
not need to be an eyewitness to do that. A recent con-
vert could do it just as well. What the eyewitness would
be expected to give (and this was the reason for the welcome accorded to him) was historical information about
this man concerning whom the kerygma made such mighty
claims.

It is often asserted that Paul had no interest in the
historical Jesus. Professor Trevor Roper, for instance, in
the article already referred to, wrote: "What concrete
facts did Paul record about the life of the Founder? None
at all." As we have already seen, this is just not true.
There is quite a solid nucleus of information about Jesus
embedded in his letters. But even if Paul, for one reason
or another, did not make many specific references to
the historical facts about Jesus, it is quite clear that others
wanted the information, and the appearance of the gospels
is the immediate proof of this. The fact that the early
Church demanded such writings as the gospels proves con-
clusively their interest in history, and any claims to the
contrary need to be fully proved and not just stated as
a fact, as if they had already been proved.

Clearly the kerygma was soon felt to be seriously in-

complete without some account of that which set it all
going. Indeed, even the kerygma itself appears to have
included some reference to the character and work of
Jesus in his earthly ministry. Acts 2:14-39 is usually regarded as a good sample of kerygmatic preaching, and
this includes a reference to "Jesus of Nazareth, a man
approved of God unto you by mighty works and wonders
which God did by him in the midst of you" (2:22). Another
affirmation of the kerygma is found in Acts 10:36-43, and
this includes the statement that the work of Jesus "began
in Galilee after the baptism that John preached." Jesus
is spoken of as "coming from Nazareth," and we are told
how "God anointed him with the Holy Spirit and with
Power. He went about doing good and healing all who
were oppressed by the devil, because God was with him.
And we are witnesses of all things which he did both in
the country of the Jews and in Jerusalem." The gospels
are the amplification of these all too brief historical references, which so far from satisfying the early Christians,
served rather to kindle their curiosity and make them
hungry for more. The gospels seem to be the answer to
this hunger.

Nor is it true that the first evangelists and the early
Christians totally lacked all historical sense, and merely
read back a kerygmatic Christ into a fictitious historical
background. The historical background of the synoptic
gospels is in fact strikingly accurate. In Mark Jesus is very
far from being merely a reflection of the risen Lord
of the kerygma. Though others in Mark's gospel occasionally and tentatively raise the possibility of his being the
Messiah, no hint of this is heard from the lips of Jesus
himself. This complete absence of any messianic claim
gives a most emphatic impression of historical accuracy
rather than of kerygmatic affirmation with no regard for
history. Further, the relationship of the followers of Jesus
to him is never referred to, as it is in the epistles, as
"incorporation into Christ" or as "believers." They are always "disciples," a word totally absent from the epistles
of the New Testament, and one that seems to have dropped

quickly out of current use long before Mark's gospel was written. This again is evidence of a certain historical sense rather than of a total indifference to the factual past in the interests of kerygmatic proclamation.

These facts and many others that point to a real historical sense in the gospel writers will have to be dealt with more fully later. This brief reference is included now to give some substance to the claim we make that what the gospels provide is not just a mythical scaffolding on which the kerygma may be supported, but to a considerable degree factual information about the human life of Jesus.

It seems particularly odd to find modern writers almost casually dismissing the idea that the early Christians had any interest in history when Luke in the opening words of his gospel explicitly insists that this is one of his primary concerns, a concern that he clearly knows is shared by many of his readers. He writes: "Many writers have undertaken to draw up an account of the events that have happened among us, following the traditions handed down to us by the original eyewitnesses and servants of the Gospel. And so in my turn . . . as one who has gone over the whole course of events in detail, I have decided to write a connected narrative for you, so as to give you authentic knowledge about the matters of which you have been informed" (NEB). Unmistakably for Luke accurate knowledge of the facts of the story of Jesus was of fundamental importance.

And it is of fundamental importance for us also. Would Paul's letters today have been of any value to us if they had not been preceded in the New Testament by the predominantly factual material of the gospels? Their theology and Christology would have sounded like empty and irrelevant dogma without the personal content provided for the word "Christ" in the gospels. Without the gospels the Christian faith becomes merely a beautiful idea, not a fact of history. For the early Christians it is quite clear that this was not adequate. They felt the need to have their faith rooted in the fact of history. That is why the gospels were written.

(2) The historical Jesus is more fundamental than the kerygma.

Some scholars have made light of the historical account of the life of Jesus in the gospels on the ground that it is subsequent to the kerygma and a consequence of it. The kerygma, they claim, is the basic fact, and the so-called historical narratives of the gospels an attempt to supply a later need that arose as a result of the kerygma. The kerygma is primary; the historical record secondary.

This seems a curious way of relating these two items. Was it not the historical fact that was primary and itself the cause of the kerygma, rather than the other way around? Those who formulated the kerygma and proclaimed it with convincing power were at first the very people who had known Jesus of Nazareth best. The kerygma was their corporate response to the impulse provided by the life and teaching of Jesus as it was consummated in his death and resurrection. Though the *writing* of the history came later than the proclamation, the history itself came first and provided the fact to which the kerygma was the response, a response born out of insight into the significance of the fact. Without its base in history the kerygma floats like an unanchored, unstable balloon. It is not the kerygma which is God's revelation to us, but the fact behind it and what men were enabled to recognize in the fact.

(3) A third reason for stressing the importance of the historical foundation to the Christian faith is this: the factuality of Jesus was something that the Church of the first two centuries refused to abandon. They saw it as something far too precious to be lost. It could have avoided opposition and won a wider measure of approval had it been willing to. If the Church today agreed to be content, as Harvey argued it might, with the "image of Jesus" as presented in the gospels, even though it had to be regarded as largely mythical or parabolic rather than historical, it would be agreeing that Christianity should fall

into the same category as the mystery religions, which were the main rivals of Christianity in the first two centuries. They had stories about great heroes, some of whom died and came back to life again; they prescribed rituals to provide for their worshipers a means of rebirth and escape from mortality. The myths about Isis, Osiris, Mythras, even in a less popular form the myth about Prometheus, embodied lofty ideas by which men's minds could be ennobled and elevated.

From the beginning, however, and with the most stubborn insistence, the early Church refused to see itself as another mystery religion. It felt itself to be based not just on a splendid thought, but on a real life and a real death through which God had become immediately real to men and in which God's will had become uniquely clear. Even the fourth gospel, which of the four most allows the Eternal Christ to be superimposed onto the historical Christ, nevertheless insists with the greatest emphasis: "The Word became flesh."

Not only was the early Church determined not to be confused with the prevalent and popular mystery religions; it equally resisted those who later tried to accommodate it to prevailing philosophic thought by eliminating its firm base in history and by arguing that the humanity of Jesus was only an "appearance," since God was such that he could not conceivably have subjected himself to such human miseries as Jesus was said to have suffered. This "Docetism," as it was called, was resisted by the Church as a very serious error, and was indeed condemned as a dangerous and impermissible distortion of the true faith. Those who today seem willing to abandon the historical element in Christianity are coming dangerously near to the docetic interpretation which the early Church felt threatened the very center of its faith.

We should therefore agree with Zahrnt when he writes: "Here then (in the gospels) we have not the eternal event of myth, but unique, unrepeatable history, not an idea but a happening, not a cultic drama but history in earnest."[3]

---

[3] The Historical Jesus, p. 65.

We agree also with Kähler: "The picture of Jesus, so full of life, so singularly beyond invention, is not the idealizing creation of the human mind; here his own being has left its imperishable impression."[4]

(4) Some scholars have written as though the mere *fact* of the incarnation is all we need to know, that God came in Christ and Christ died on a cross. But to most Christians, if the incarnation is to mean anything we need to know what it was like as well as the fact that it happened. Moreover, the death of Jesus, to which Christian faith has attached the utmost importance, is irrelevant and purposeless apart from the character and quality of the one who died, and the reasons for which he died. For full Christian faith, therefore, it is essential that we should know all that can be learned of the "how" of the incarnation, as well as the mere fact of it.

Bultmann's position of extreme historical skepticism toward the materials in the gospels seems to us, therefore, not only to go far beyond what is required by the facts of the case, but is in some danger of making light of what the Christian faith at crucial moments in its history has regarded as essential.

It is a matter of extreme interest that several of Bultmann's distinguished pupils, now in their own right New Testament scholars of the highest rank, who at one time largely shared Bultmann's attitude in this matter, have as a result of their own further studies in the gospels felt compelled to abandon their master's extreme position in favor of an attitude more open to both the possibility of historical knowledge about Jesus and also the importance of it. Characteristic quotations from the writings of two of them will suffice for the moment. Käsemann, whose essay on *The Problem of the Historical Jesus* (1953) was one of the first signs of this new concern, wrote there: "I am not prepared to concede that defeatism or scepticism must have the last word and lead to complete lack of interest in the earthly Jesus. . . . Some characteristic

---

[4] *Historische Jesus*, p. 78.

features of Jesus emerge with a reasonable clarity." Born-kamm, not without significance, entitled his book on this theme *Jesus of Nazareth* and in it spoke of "the main historical, indisputable traits" (p. 53) in Jesus that are recognizable in the gospels: "The gospels in fact bring before our eyes the historical person of Jesus with the utmost vividness.... What the gospels report concerning the message, deeds and history of Jesus is still distinguished by an authenticity, a freshness, a distinctiveness not in any way effaced by the Church's Easter Faith. These features point us directly to the earthly figure of Jesus" (p. 24). Professor Trevor Roper also, who speaks of the "palpable rubbish" in the gospels, nevertheless concedes that "behind the gospels we detect a personality too strong, too individual, too consistent to have been invented."

It is this figure "beyond invention" concerning whom we wish to find out all we can, since information as full and accurate as possible is of the greatest significance for Christian faith and discipleship.

Chapter 5

Evidence of Historicity in the Gospels

We are not attempting to claim that every item in the gospels is historically accurate, but we do claim that the influence of faith upon them has not destroyed beyond recovery the historical record in them. The last chapter ended with quotations to this effect from Käsemann and Bornkamm, and we begin this one with similar quotations from the same authors. Bornkamm writes: "If the gospels do not speak of the history of Jesus as a chronological account of his life with its outward and inward development, yet none the less they speak of history as occurrence and event. Of such history the gospels provide information which is more than abundant" (*Jesus of Nazareth*, p. 25). Käsemann writes more cautiously but still emphatically: "There are pieces in the synoptic tradition which the historian must simply acknowledge as authentic, if he wishes to remain a historian" (*Essays on New Testament Themes*, p. 213). Nineham, whose approach is usually that of Bultmann, also agrees that "we can often be virtually sure that what the tradition is offering us are the authentic deeds and especially the authentic words of the historic Jesus" (*Commentary on Mark*, p. 51).

What features of the gospels, when taken as a whole, confirm this impression of authenticity?

J. B. Phillips, whose translation of Paul's letters into modern English (entitled *Letters to Young Churches*) was a brilliant piece of work, later spent some years working on the translation of the gospels as well. Some time afterwards he wrote a book called *The Ring of Truth*, in which he dealt with this subject of the historical reliability of the gospels. He gave a number of reasons why the gospels as a whole may be regarded as basically reliable, but his appeal was mainly to what he called this "Ring of Truth" which one sensed as one read them. He argued that when someone has been long in their company, as he had, he comes to develop a kind of intuitive sense of what in them is genuinely historical and what is not. This may well be true, and a considerable degree of such sensitivity may well have formed itself in his own mind as his work on the gospels continued. But this personal sense of certainty does not carry over to other people merely by asserting it, unless the people concerned are ready to place unquestioning faith in one's intuitive judgment, or unless one can provide objective tests to support his "hunch."

C. H. Dodd's judgment on New Testament questions is widely treated with the deepest respect. His book *The Founder of Christianity*, therefore, with its modest but confident portrait of the historical figure of Jesus, brought great reassurance to many readers. The subtitles given to the book were not equally accurate descriptions of the book's contents. "What do we really know about Jesus?" was the first, and one could not complain of that. But the second subtitle was: "How do we know it?"

This was somewhat misleading because Professor Dodd's book did not pursue this part of the inquiry. Certainly he indicated some of the grounds on which his judgments were based, but they were not worked out systematically. So the book's main value was that it gave the reader the considered opinion on this most important subject of one whom very many in Great Britain regarded as the greatest living authority on the New Testament. The explanation of *how* he reached his judgment of what could firmly be believed about Jesus was not, however, a prominent feature of the book.

Our present aim, therefore, is to try to provide persuasive arguments for a belief in the historical trustworthiness of much in the synoptic gospels rather than to appeal to what "sounds right" to us, though we may not be able wholly to avoid something of this second approach as well.

We remind readers that we are not trying to prove everything in the synoptics historically accurate. Some materials in them we should agree come unmistakably from the later faith of the Church. Some of these items have already been mentioned. Others that may be noted in passing are such items as these: (i) The splendid closing words of Matthew's gospel (Matt. 28:18-20) with their reference to baptism in the name of the Father, Son, and Holy Spirit. (ii) The detailed wording of the third prediction of the passion by Jesus in Mark 10:33-34, which includes so many of the particular items that are later recorded as actually taking place: an initial condemnation by Jewish authorities, execution by command of the Roman governor, the mocking, spitting, and scourging. (iii) The saying about Peter's being the rock on which the Church will be built (Matt. 16:18), since this occurs only in Matthew and uses the word "church" (*ekklesia*), which occurs in no other gospel, but which became a very important word in the life of the post-Easter Church. (iv) The details that Matthew adds (in 28:1-4) to Mark's account of the discovery of the empty tomb by the women—the earthquake, the angel rolling away the stone, his dazzling garments (cf. Mark 16:1-2). A considerable number of similar items could be added and reasons given why they must be suspect as reliable historical records.

We fully recognize also that all the materials of these three gospels had first been told and retold orally, before they were eventually written down, by men who believed in Jesus as the Son of God and wanted others to come to that same belief as a result of what they reported and wrote. Their high veneration for Jesus may well have affected the way they told their story. Their desire sometimes to indicate the significance of what they reported may have led at times to distortion.

We find it difficult to believe, however, that the story as a whole was distorted to a degree that totally obscures the basic facts. The time between the death of Jesus and the writing of the gospels was not long enough for such total distortion to have taken place. Between the death of Jesus and the writing of Mark there was an interval of about thirty years—a comparatively short time. Some scholars have treated the gospel narratives as if they belonged to the same class of folk tales as the stories of the Old Testament patriarchs, arguing from the way these developed to the way the gospel material must have been adapted. But this provides no real comparison at all. The stories of the patriarchs were repeated over and over again during a period of several centuries. By the time they came to be written down, not decades but centuries had passed since the death of the last possible eyewitness. Over such a long period and with no person still alive to provide any check on accuracy, much modification could take place. But in the case of Mark's gospel the interval is only thirty years, and thirty years is a very short period of time. To a boy of twelve it is true that thirty years seems like an age; but for the man of sixty the events of his life thirty years before, especially outstanding events such as contact with Jesus must have been, stand out as clearly as yesterday's. Indeed, it is commonly said that a man of seventy can recall remarkable events and people of forty years before even better than he remembers similar events of the previous year. Even in the period of thirty years some events can of course be embellished, but not out of all recognition of the original facts. One reason given by Professor Roper for not dismissing the gospel records as totally unreliable is that it would seem unlikely that "Christ was invented out of nothing and located, with such precision, *in so recent a past*" (italics ours). We hope at a later stage to emphasize the point he makes in his phrase "located with such precision." At the moment we echo his recognition of the difficulty of dismissing it all as make-believe when it deals with "so recent a past."

We recall also the point made earlier that there is evidence that in the early Church a word attributed to Jesus was treated with great respect and not subjected to careless distortion. We saw how Paul quoted a known word of Jesus to provide an authoritative solution to a moral problem, and was at considerable pains to insist that his own advice, even when he felt he had the guidance of the Spirit, was at a much lower level of authority. Similarly, he records the words of Jesus at the Last Supper (I Cor. 11:24) as though he is passing on a precious treasure that must not be sullied in any way by careless reporting. We saw, too, Luke's insistence (Luke 1:1-2) on the care he has taken to discover historically reliable material and to pass it on accurately.

We offer six further considerations that suggest that in general the synoptic gospels can be regarded as providing valuable historical evidence as well as being most effective affirmations of faith:

(1) The first point is the striking difference between the synoptic gospels and those we call "apocryphal." The latter strike us as clearly imaginative exaggerations or else plain inventions in the direction of heightening the miraculous deeds of Jesus or his theological status. They do not commend themselves to us as historical material, and the early Church had such a clear sense of what was appropriate that it rejected them from its canon.

The features of the synoptic gospels, which distinguish them so sharply from the apocryphal gospels, are precisely of a kind to indicate that the synoptics are much nearer to recording what actually happened—much nearer. They offer, compared with the fantasy of the apocryphal gospels, what reads like sober, factual reporting.

It may be well to give one or two instances of what religious imagination uncontrolled by fact can accomplish:

(a) In the Gospel to the Hebrews there occurs: "The Saviour himself said: 'Even now did my mother the Holy Spirit take me by one of my hairs and carried me away to the great mountain Tabor.' "

(b) In a document known as The Gospel of Thomas (not the document of that name recently found at Nag Hammadi, which consists almost entirely of sayings attributed to Jesus) we find the following:

(i) "Now Jesus made twelve sparrows of clay on the Sabbath. Joseph said: 'Why do you profane the Sabbath?' Jesus looked on the sparrows and said: 'Go, take your flight.' They took flight and went up into the air."

(ii) "A child running through a village dashed against the shoulder of Jesus. Jesus, provoked, said: 'Thou shalt not finish thy course.' And immediately he fell down and died."

(iii) "When he was six years old Jesus broke a pitcher in which he was to have fetched water. So he spread his garment on the ground and carried the water to his mother in it."

(iv) Joseph cut two beams for a bed, and one was shorter than the other. Jesus miraculously lengthened it to match the other.

(c) In the Gospel of Peter we read: "The soldiers saw three men come out of the sepulchre, two of them sustaining the other and a cross following them. Of the two their heads reached to heaven, but the head of him that was led by them overpassed the heavens. And they heard a voice out of the heavens saying: 'Hast thou preached unto them that sleep?' And an answer was heard from the cross, saying: 'Yes.' "

(d) In the Arabic Gospel of the Infancy this occurs: "When Jesus passes the trees bow to give him fruit."

Here and there even in the canonical four gospels a very improbable story with something of the flavor of these apocryphal stories has managed to gain a place—such as the episode about the coin in the fish's mouth, Peter walking on the water, or the very large quantities of water being changed into wine at Cana. Matthew and John appear to be most susceptible to this pressure toward exaggeration. Taken as a whole, however, our four gospels, and especially the synoptics, are in a totally different world from that of the apocryphals, and the difference is that the synoptics are unmistakably much nearer to fact. Fact exercises little control over the apocryphal. It maintains a very considerable control in the synoptics.

(2) A less startling difference, but still a very obvious one, exists between the fourth gospel and Mark. From very early days this difference was recognized and John's was known as the "spiritual gospel," because it sat loose to the facts of history and aimed primarily at bringing out the spiritual significance of the story of Jesus. Sometimes John declares boldly deep truths about Jesus as being evident during his earthly ministry, which are entirely missing from, or at most only implicit in, the synoptics. Sometimes, to make his theological point more clearly, he adapts and modifies what is historical to make it serve his purposes. For instance, in John, Jesus, even at the very beginning of his ministry, makes no secret of the fact that he is and knows himself to be the Messiah. The significance of Jesus himself dominates all the teaching in John, to the exclusion of the Kingdom of God, which is dominant throughout the synoptics. The word attributed to Jesus: "Before Abraham was, I am," is not likely to be a historical saying of the human Jesus, though it expresses the growing faith of the Church in his pre-existence. The well-known and much-loved "I" sayings enshrine eternal truths about Christ that are very precious to Christians: "I am the Way, the Truth and the Life," "I and the Father are one," etc.; but they enshrine eternal truths of spiritual significance rather than reproduce the actual words of Jesus during his earthly ministry.

Moreover, in the fourth gospel Jesus is represented as speaking in long theological discourses. One of them continues throughout three chapters (15 to 17). He also uses theological or even semi-philosophical words to explain himself and his message; and words more appropriate to the post-resurrection period are attributed to the human Jesus: "Abide in me and I in you."

In the synoptics, however, especially in Mark, we find something quite different. The theme of the preaching of Jesus is not the person of Jesus himself but the Kingdom of God. This phrase fills the gospel of Mark, but occurs only twice, almost casually, in John. In Mark the sayings of Jesus consist largely of short, pithy sentences made up of homely words from the farm, the countryside, or the peasant household—seeds, birds, dogs, camels, children, cups, needles, salt, wallets, beds, etc. There are no long discourses, only the vivid stories embedded in the common life of Palestine which we know as parables. There is no instance in Mark where Jesus speaks of himself as Messiah or even clearly acknowledges the title as applicable to himself. In the older translations Mark 14:62 reads like an acknowledgment. But this may not represent the oldest form of the text. Some scholars think that the actual answer of Jesus before the courts may well have been nearer to the form given to it in Matthew 26:64: "The word is yours" (NEB). This list of differences between Mark and John could be greatly extended. They are sufficient, however, to make the point that John sits loose to history as he elaborates his "spiritual" gospel. In comparison Mark keeps close to history. Mark believed that what he reported was what happened, and that God's truth had come to men through the man Jesus. John felt that the eternal truth had for many been so obscured during the earthly life of Jesus that it was his task to make plain what had in fact at that time been hidden.

These striking differences between John and Mark are almost entirely due to the fact that Mark keeps very much closer to history than John. This entitles us to regard Mark as a source from which historical material can be derived.

(3) A third indication of Mark's historical reliability is his accurate presentation of the social, historical, and geographical conditions in Palestine in the early part of the first century A.D. These are introduced casually as the

background to the stories about Jesus. Their remarkable accuracy is not consistent with the picture sometimes painted of Mark as one who was allowing the faith of the later Church to distort and mold the whole of his narrative. They rather give the impression of overall accuracy, as of one who reports faithfully what actually happened. So we gain from Mark a reliably accurate understanding of the position and status at the time of Jesus of the temple at Jerusalem, with its various courts, the presence of the local synagogue in every town, the various pressure groups within the community—Pharisees, Sadducees, scribes, Herod, Pilate, priests and "high priests," Samaritans and Gentiles. What we learn about the regulations concerning the sabbath, ritual cleanliness, and diet restrictions corresponds to what we learn from other historical sources. Would a writer whose main concern it was merely to present the faith of the post-resurrection Church have achieved such a degree of background accuracy? This information comes over accurately because it is Mark's intention to reproduce everything accurately.

The local geography also is presented correctly—Jerusalem, Jericho, Bethany, the Mount of Olives, Nazareth, Capernaum, Bethsaida, Tyre and Sidon to the north, and the Decapolis to the east of the river Jordan.

Again the social and agricultural life of the time comes through with remarkable accuracy and consistency. Jeremias, who has made a special study of this, and who wrote an important book entitled *Jerusalem at the Time of Jesus*, has shown in his book on the parables how accurately they reflect the social life of the times. The parable of the Sower implies the actual conditions of farming at that time. Mark's story of the man let down through the roof of a house into the very presence of Jesus inside fits in with what is known of the Palestinian house of that time. Luke, by contrast, introduces a reference to "tiles," reading his knowledge of what houses in Greek cities were like back into the Palestinian situation, and in the process making the story sound very improbable.

Mark's representation of the popular beliefs about demons as the cause of all kinds of evils is true to that time. It is interesting, by comparison, to note that John avoids these references to demon-possession.

The common language in southern Palestine at that time was a form of Aramaic, a language akin to Hebrew. Aramaic appears in somewhat different dialects in different areas of Palestine and the surrounding countries. Mark's representation of Peter as recognizable as a northerner by his dialect (14:70) sounds very probable—just as a Scotsman can be recognized by his manner of speech in England. Jesus would speak Aramaic normally, though he may also have had a working knowledge of Greek. Many Jews did at that time. Mark's gospel itself appears to have been written in Greek by one whose natural language was Aramaic, and much of the teaching material of Jesus appears to come from an Aramaic original, although in the gospels it comes to us, of course, in Greek. Aramaic scholars point out the frequency of the "divine passive," where a passive voice is used to avoid introducing the name of God as subject. When some of the words of Jesus are translated back into Aramaic, scholars can find in them evidence of rhythm, alliteration, and assonance. This Aramaic background to the teaching of Jesus and to Mark's own style of writing is all favorable to historical accuracy as against later invention.

Moreover, Mark records the actual Aramaic words that Jesus used on one or two specially memorable occasions: his cry from the cross, "Eloi, Eloi, lama sabachthani"; his words that awoke the little girl thought to be dead, "Talitha Cumi"; the shout that penetrated the almost total deafness of the man whose faith had to be awakened by the visible use of saliva, "Ephphatha"; "Golgotha," the local name for the place of Jesus' execution.

All this local knowledge of Palestine comes in so naturally that it is impossible to think it was fathered onto the story by a Christian of a later generation in order to give verisimilitude to his theological reconstructions. Fact rather than faith put it there. This is what Trevor Roper meant when he spoke of Christ being "located" in the gospels "with such precision."

(4) The teaching of Jesus will be mentioned only briefly here, since it will be considered more fully in a later chapter. This teaching, however, has such a large degree of coherence and such a large measure of striking originality and individuality that the main bulk of it must come from one single mind with a most remarkable penetration and insight into religious and moral truth. The parables as a whole bear the stamp of a single mind. Many of the words of Jesus reflect something of the poetic structure of the prophetic parts of the Old Testament. Certain mannerisms constantly recur, for instance, a rather frequent use of threefoldness in the teaching materials and a surprising frequency in the use of the question. The symbols by which deep truths are conveyed consist of objects drawn from the everyday life of the Palestinian peasant, including a specially large number of living creatures and plants. There is a notable absence of theological words and the technical terms of religion.

All this points to one great mind as its source. Communities would not create teaching with such a large degree of consistency in form and mannerism as well as content.

(5) In the handing on of narratives over a comparatively short period, what usually happens is that the essential core of the narrative remains basically the same, though details attached to it may be lost or changed, or others may come to be added. Dr. Vincent Taylor, while a tutor at Headingley College, Leeds, at the time when Form Criticism was first becoming known in Great Britain, carried out an interesting experiment. He read the report of an incident to a small group of students. After an interval each of these students was asked to write down this narrated incident and then reread it to another small group of students—each student to a different group. After another interval each one of the second group of students was asked to recount it to still others. The versions of the

final hearers were then compared with the original story and also with the story in its intermediate stages.

It was found that in general the story tended to become briefer as it was told, though not in every case; names tended to be omitted; details were changed. But the nucleus of the story remained recognizably the same. And this is probably substantially what happened with many of the stories about Jesus. They retained the essential point, but were subject to variation in detail. Too much should not therefore be built upon the details of a gospel narrative, but its main thrust probably has historical foundation.

(6) The last of the general considerations that we wish to mention as favoring a historical basis to the synoptic gospels is the very noticeable absence from them of those concerns which, so far as we can estimate the matter, were the predominant interest of the early Church. So far from these interests being foisted back upon the gospels, they are remarkably absent from them, or nearly so.

We have already noted that Mark carefully refrains from any suggestion that Jesus ever referred to himself as Messiah. We have also noted that the followers of Jesus are constantly called "disciples"; yet this is a word that totally disappeared from the epistles of the New Testament, in favor of other descriptive names.

The word "church," so prominent in Paul's letters and in the book of Revelation, occurs only twice in the synoptic gospels, and both these occasions are in material peculiar to Matthew. The Lord's Supper, which appears to have been a very important feature of the life of the early Church, plays no part in the synoptic gospels except in the episode of the Last Supper. Similarly, baptism is hardly present, except in a metaphorical sense for some distressing ordeal, and in connection with the baptism of Jesus by John the Baptist.

The Holy Spirit fills the pages both of Acts and of the letters of Paul, but not of the synoptics. It is true the phrase occurs occasionally, but it is rare in the gospels —far rarer than one would expect if the faith of the early Church had created the gospels without any effective control from history.

The absence from the synoptic gospels of the words and concerns that were dominant in the early Church and the consistent use of others that had in fact dropped out of use within thirty years of the death of Jesus clearly lead to the belief that the facts of history for the synoptic writers were not by any means carelessly overridden in the interests of the later faith.

On these grounds, therefore, it is not unreasonable to claim that the matters presented in the synoptic gospels have a considerable degree of historical reality within them. Later faith may have influenced them, but it has not changed them beyond recognition.

Chapter 6

Criteria for Distinguishing
Historical from Nonhistorical

We have seen that there are good reasons for believing
that the synoptic gospels retain a good deal of historical
material, even though the influence of the later faith of
the Church is recognizable in some of the features that
are present. Can we devise tests by which the historical
elements can be distinguished from those which are but
expressions of faith? We concede that these tests do not
provide final and unanswerable proof. Such proof is no
longer available to us. But grounds for strong probability
can be worked out, and it is these which we now try to
outline.

(1) The first may be called the test of "multiple attestation." This is similar to the test that is used as one
means of determining the correct reading of a text in a
disputed passage where different manuscripts give different readings. If one reading can be shown to be present
in the manuscripts that are regarded as the earliest and
most reliable, and if these manuscripts can also be shown
to come from different areas of manuscript tradition, then
the reading has a very strong claim to be regarded as

the original reading. Readings found only in texts of late origin, or which are supported by only one manuscript or by only one family of manuscripts, are regarded as much less likely to be original.

A similar method can be used in relation to the search for the historical element in the gospels. In fact it was predominantly this test which the early researchers into the Jesus of history fifty years ago used as their basic method. We have seen that behind the synoptic gospels there are recognizable sources, probably all of a written kind. Mark is the earliest of the gospels, usually dated about A.D. 65, and this is a basic source, used later by both Matthew and Luke. The sayings collection, which was also used by both Matthew and Luke and usually called "Q," must also be of an early date since it was available to Matthew and Luke independently and in presumably different areas of the ancient world. This is the second basic source. Scholars have also regarded the matter peculiar to Luke's gospel as of early origin. It is customary today to be exceedingly skeptical of any conventional explanation of its origin, but the usual explanation of L used to be that it consisted of the material that Luke was able to collect on the spot while he was Paul's companion during his imprisonment in Palestine prior to his commitment for trial in Rome. (The basis of this understanding is Acts 21:17 and 27:1, where it is reported that Luke was with Paul on his arrival in Jerusalem, and still with him when he was to be sent to Rome.) If indeed this were so, then Luke's special material is both early in date and reliable in its origin. We noted also that some scholars are persuaded, because of the way in which Luke has used his Markan source, that he had already combined what he took from Q and L into a kind of "first draft" before Mark became available to him. Mark was then used to supplement what was already prepared. This would give L a date not later than Mark, at any rate if it was available to Luke before he knew Mark. Whatever grounds may be given for the opinion, it is widely believed that L may be regarded as a third early and independent source.

There is also M, the material peculiar to Matthew. The narratives in this peculiarly Matthean source are regarded as the least reliable of all in the synoptics, and most scholars would date this source as later than the other three. It adds authority when it confirms what is in the other three, but in its narrative material at any rate it would not be regarded as a reliable source at points where it is unsupported by others. The chief primary sources are therefore three in number: Mark, Q, and L.

If an item occurs in any one of these early sources, it has a presumptive right to be considered as probably historical in essence; if it occurs in two of these three independent sources, that right is greatly strengthened, since it means it is supported by two early and independent witnesses. If it is supported by all three, then its attestation is extremely strong.

M and the fourth gospel have to be treated with caution as historical sources, but where they support what is found in one or more of the three primary sources, that support can be regarded as adding further strength to their evidence. If they are alone in their attestation, it must normally be treated with reserve. Luke's and Matthew's variations from Mark would not usually be regarded as historical, but examples of the influence of the beliefs of the later Church.

By the use of this proposed test of "multiple attestation," we find that quite a number of items can claim threefold or even quadruple support from these early sources. Professor H. K. McArthur summarized the evidence as follows:

> Some of the motifs supported by all four strands of the synoptics (or at least three including Mark and Q) are the following: proclamations of the Kingdom of God; the presence of disciples; healing miracles; a link with John the Baptist; the use of parables; concern for outcasts, especially the "tax-gatherers and sinners"; illustrations of a radi-

cal ethic; the love commandment; the demand that the disciples practise forgiveness; clashes with his contemporaries over sabbath observance; sayings about the Son of Man; the use of "Amen" to introduce Jesus' logia (*Expository Times,* January 1971, p. 118).

To these may be added the fact that Jesus gave missionary directions to his disciples, with the obvious implication that he had disciples and that he sent them out on missionary work.

This list of items, with a strong claim to historicity on the basis of this particular test, makes a solid nucleus with which to begin.

(2) A second criterion is this: Since it appears almost certain that the fourth gospel was written independently of the synoptics, representing the transmission of the original tradition through an entirely separate channel, this gives some value to the evidence of the fourth gospel, which at one time was regarded as valueless from a historical point of view. What the author of the fourth gospel gives in the way of apparently historical information has to be treated with the utmost reserve, if his testimony is at variance with or unsupported by anything in the synoptic tradition. When, however, he provides information that is in line with that of the synoptics, this may now be treated as independent confirmation. This test gives support to a number of historical items that occur in one or other of the primary sources, but not all of them. These include the cleansing of the temple by Jesus; the influence of the ex-high priest Annas at the time of the trial of Jesus; Pilate's attempt to achieve the release of Jesus as a gesture of clemency, but his failure as a result of the crowd's demand for Barabbas; and the fact that on the cross the crime of Jesus was described in the words "King of the Jews."

(3) The third test is associated with what used to be called "the stumbling-block characteristics of Jesus," those aspects of his character and message which were offensive to even the most sincere among the Jews of his time, and even to the followers of Jesus at a later time.

He himself is reported as saying: "Blessed is he who finds no offence [stumbling block] in me." Here may be listed such things as the attitude of Jesus to the sabbath, fasting, and divorce (in contradiction to Moses' authorization of it in certain conditions), his free-and-easy relationships with people not regarded as respectable, the non-ascetic characteristics that led to his being called "a gluttonous man and a winebibber," his insistence on the generous, undemanding offer of God's forgiveness and on God's expectation that man should offer glad and unrestricted forgiveness to his fellow man, and the fact that on occasion Jesus showed anger. These items which the early Church found embarrassing are not likely to have been the invention of the early Church.

(4) The fourth and final test is a recent development of the one just discussed. It is often referred to as the test of "dissimilarity." This test, when applied rigorously, is an excessively restrictive criterion, but the small nucleus of items it allows has an extremely strong claim to authenticity, though to use it to exclude all others would be totally unjustifiable.

This test argues that only those items in the records about Jesus may be regarded as historical which could not have arisen within contemporary Judaism nor within the early Christian community. If they could have come from either of these sources, then, it is claimed, the probability is that they did. In fact this is very similar to test (3), but since it is the form in which recent scholarship has formulated it, it seems best to treat it separately. The items that are authenticated by this test correspond very closely to those named under the "stumbling-block" characteristics.

This very strict test may provide, as we agreed, an unassailable nucleus, but it is going beyond all reasonable bounds to argue that nothing else about Jesus may be regarded as historical if it is not covered by this test. Almost certainly Jesus, like the Old Testament prophets before him, accepted much that was good from his nation's past or from contemporary thought and practice,

and equally certainly much that the early Church believed and practiced would be accepted on the very
ground that they believed it to represent aspects of the
teaching and attitudes of Jesus.

If, for instance, we argued that only that could be
genuinely true about Luther which was both different
from the Catholic Church of his time and also from the
Lutheran Church that sprang out of his work, it would
leave us with a very attenuated and totally inadequate
picture of Luther. Similarly, if we were restricted to accepting as true about John Wesley only those things in
which he differed from the Church of England of his
time and also from the early Methodists who were formed
into a society as a result of his work, we should have a
very odd, and far from historical, picture of the man. So
with Jesus. This stringent test provides a solid nucleus of
historical material, but a nucleus to which must be added
elements that he took over from the best in the traditions
of his people and elements that the continuing life of
the Church adopted because they had his authority.

We believe, therefore, that there is much genuinely
historical material in the gospels, and that the tests enu-
merated provide reasonably objective criteria by which
authentic material can be separated from non-authentic.
On the basis of such tests as these we proceed to try to
identify the elements in the gospels that may, without
credulity, be accepted as historical, and those which must
be eliminated as nonhistorical. In between these two
groups will lie a considerable amount of material concerning which these tests do not enable us to reach any
clear judgment.

In these cases there is one other test that may be
applicable. It is the test of consistency. Is the item under
discussion wholly consistent with the solid nucleus of
historical material provided by the tests? Sometimes this
has been called the test of "co-inherence." There are items
that do not find strong support from the four tests just
listed which may nevertheless be accepted as authentic,

if they are seen to be wholly consistent with the total picture of Jesus reconstructed from the tests. That is probably historically true which is "all of a piece" with other historical items. That is, have they "the ring of truth" not just to one single assessor but in the presence of the other authentic material?

Chapter 7

Historical Features in the Portrait of Jesus

This chapter deals not so much with events in the ministry of Jesus or with elements in his teaching that may be accepted as historical, but with aspects of his character and bearing that can be accepted as authentic. We accept them as authentic on one or more of the following grounds: (1) They appear in more than one of the primary sources, that is, they have both early and double attestations. (2) They have something of the "stumbling-block" characteristic, in that they are items that the early Church found some difficulty in assimilating, and so cannot be suspected of inventing them. (3) They pass the test of "dissimilarity" in that they do not conform to the kind of things that might have been derived from contemporary Judaism or from early Christianity. By the use of these three tests we seek now to isolate some of those elements in the tradition that Kähler described as "beyond the power of invention." We do not pretend that what follows is an exhaustive list, but it is an impressive list, and the way the items are selected shows how the tests can be applied.

First and foremost comes the fact of the cross itself. No one, neither Jew and still less Christian, would have been likely to invent that. The Old Testament declared that God's curse rested on one who was executed in this way. The early Church appears to have found it an embarrassing fact, and only with difficulty came to terms with it. Paul asserts that to Jews the cross was a stumbling block and to Gentiles an object of ridicule, when it was claimed that God himself was involved in it. Mockers found the cross an easy target for their jibes, and Christians did not find it easy to parry them. Nothing but the grim and inescapable fact that Jesus died on a cross can explain its presence in the Christian tradition. Jewish expectation had no place for such painful humiliation in their looked-for Messiah.

That Jesus was executed on a cross means also that Jesus was executed not by the Jewish authorities, but by the Roman, since they alone used the method of crucifixion. Moreover, the charges on which he was condemned to such a horrible death must have been understood by the Romans as constituting a potential threat to their security. This in its turn would make probable the report in the gospels that by some people at any rate he was spoken of as a Messiah, since an association with messianic expectations would, in common understanding, imply dangerous patriotic fervor and antagonism to foreign rulers.

Similarly, the baptism of Jesus at the hands of John the Baptist must be accepted as historical. No Jew would have thought of inventing it and certainly no Christian would have felt it appropriate. Nothing in Jewish expectations would have led anyone to anticipate John's unusual practice of baptizing Jews, as a means or a sign of spiritual renewal. It was proper enough for proselytes, but not for Jews. For Christians, too, it was a source of embarrassment, since everyone assumed that it was the greater person who baptized the lesser. Moreover, John's baptism was associated with repentance for past wrong-doing, as well as with an intention to make a new start. In the case of Jesus both these implications were unacceptable to the early Christians. They believed that Jesus was far greater than John, and also that he was without sin and so in no need of a baptism implying repentance. Indeed, Matthew 3:14-15 is usually understood as a contrivance of the early Church to suggest a reason why the sinless Jesus should submit himself to John for baptism. John is represented as protesting: "I need rather to be baptized by you." And it is implied that Jesus felt no repentance, but explained his action as an unusual fulfilment in special circumstances of God's will. Some of the apocryphal gospels make further attempts to deal with the taunt that Jesus' baptism implied on his part a confession of sin. Because of the very difficulties it created for the Christians, the baptism of Jesus could not conceivably have been invented by them for theological reasons.

Similarly, the almost casual bit of information that Mark slips in at 6:3 to the effect that Jesus was a carpenter is not likely to have been invented. Even in Mark it is used by critics as a kind of sneer, as though it can be taken as obvious that one from such a humble background could not be expected to be a person of great spiritual significance. One has the impression, too, that Matthew's slight modification of Mark's blunt comment betrays something of the embarrassment the early Church came to feel in the matter. Matthew changes Mark's "Is not this the carpenter?" to "Is not this the carpenter's son?" (Matt. 13:55), making the offensive category slightly more remote.

Also historical must be the fact that Jesus came from Nazareth, an unimportant town far to the north of Jerusalem. People of Jerusalem would think of it as Londoners think of Wigan or Oswaldwistle. It was no place anyone would invent for the birthplace of a very important person. Nazareth was a town of Galilee, a remote northern province of Jewish territory, separated from Judaea itself by a broad belt of land known as Samaria, which was occupied by people regarded as heretical and traditionally bitterly hostile to the Jews. Galilee itself was by repute far from orthodox and was felt by strict Jews to be far too open to Gentile influences. It was sneered at by southern Jews as "Gentile Galilee"—not at all the place anyone would invent as the early home of one whom the Church came to reverence as God's Messiah. Moreover, the difficulty that both Matthew and Luke felt in harmonizing the known fact that Jesus spent his early childhood in Nazareth but was reputed to have been born in Bethlehem and the fact that each tried to achieve it in a different way points to the stubborn fact of the presence of Nazareth in the earliest tradition. The link, therefore, of Jesus with Nazareth and Galilee can be regarded as historically certain.

Mark mentions quite casually the names of Jesus' mother Mary and of his brothers James, Joses, Judas, and Simon, as well as some sisters. There would seem to be no reason whatever for naming them were they not actually remembered in this way. Mark does not make any reference to anyone known as Jesus' father, but at Luke 4:22 Luke records the question: "Is not this Joseph's son?" The birth stories themselves, however, could not be accorded a very high priority in any list of historical material in the gospels. They are not found in any of the primary sources, nor are the individual facts vouched for by more than one writer. Indeed, Matthew and Luke give such totally different accounts that there are many serious discrepancies between them. But there seems no reason to doubt that Jesus' parents were called Joseph and Mary.

The fact that Mark retains some of the words spoken by Jesus in the original Aramaic makes it most probable that Aramaic was his native tongue, something that on other grounds one would expect to be the case. In addition there is the argument from Aramaic scholars that many of the sayings of Jesus betray an Aramaic original behind their Greek form in the gospels.

One feature of the ministry of Jesus that may be regarded as historically reliable is that he possessed remarkable powers of restoring ailing men and women to full health and strength. Not only is this a constantly recurring feature in all four gospels, but it is securely present in all the primary sources, as well as in M and John. It may, however, be argued that this is just the kind of material that the early Church might exaggerate or even invent and then project back onto Jesus, once they had reached the conviction that he was the Saviour of the world. But there is strong, even decisive evidence that the stories of healing did not have their origin in the later faith of the early Church. Not only is the background to the healings in many cases so true to the situation in Palestine and so not likely to come from someone's imagination, not only do all the primary sources bear independent testimony to this, but one other feature seems to be on its own quite decisive.

In southern Palestine at the time of Jesus it was the common belief that many illnesses were caused by demon-possession, especially those which had some degree of psychological abnormality attached to them. The gospel writers continually represent Jesus as having the power to exorcise demons. In particular there is one incident, recorded in all three synoptic gospels, where the enemies of Jesus gather to try to undermine his growing influence with the people. The simplest way, had it been plausible, would have been for them to deny outright the reports that Jesus healed people or cast out demons. They apparently realized, however, that such a denial was quite impossible. To attempt it would have discredited themselves rather than Jesus. The healing work of Jesus was too well known for that, and too many people were known to have benefited from his touch. Since the scribes cannot deny his power, the only way they can discredit him is by ascribing this power to an evil source. They agree, therefore, to spread the report that he gained his successes only because he was in league with the ruler of the demons: "He is possessed by Beelzebul," they said, "and by the prince of the demons he casts out demons" (Mark 3:22).

We can be sure that a story like that would not be invented by pious Christians of a later generation. Therefore it must have been a true story. But the story itself makes it quite clear that even the enemies of Jesus were

forced by the very facts of the case to admit his powers
to heal. The best they could do was to try to argue that
an evil power gave him this remarkable ability.

This also gives a strong degree of probability to the
reply of Jesus: "How can Satan cast out Satan? No one
can enter a strong man's house and plunder his goods
unless he first binds the strong man." The implication is
that Jesus felt that power had been given him to set
free men and women whom Satan had made his victims,
and the description of them as "those whom Satan had
bound" may well be the very words Jesus used to describe
those who were desperately ill or crippled (as also at
Luke 13:16).

This certainty that Jesus was in fact a healer of men's
illnesses gives *prima facie* probability to the stories of
healing as told in the gospels—not perhaps to the details
of each individual case, but to the main fact that in the
presence of Jesus people found healing.

Another feature that is beyond doubt, because it is
found in all the primary sources as well as being deeply
embedded in all four gospels, is that Jesus showed a most
unexpected and deeply resented friendship and concern
for the outcasts of society, variously described as "harlots
and tax-gatherers" or "tax-gatherers and sinners." Among
contemporary Jews it was incredible that anyone claiming
to speak as a prophet of God would degrade himself and
his message by such conduct. There was nothing in the
Jewish tradition to make people think that anyone in the
role of Messiah would act in such a way. It may even be
that some of the early Christians also lapsed into the way
of thinking of tax-gatherers and sinners as people whose
company should be avoided. At least in Matthew 18:17
there is a very odd statement that a Christian who re-
fuses to be reconciled to a fellow Christian in spite of
the representations of the church officials must as a pun-
ishment be treated as "a Gentile and a tax-gatherer." This
sounds like advice to cut him off from Christian society
and ignore him. It is most unlikely that Jesus himself
spoke like this. It is equally unlikely that a church com-

munity that had begun to think in these terms would be the kind of society that would create out of nothing the picture of Jesus as "the friend of tax-gatherers and sinners." This improbability together with the unanimity of the earliest sources makes this feature of the work of Jesus one that we can confidently accept as historical. It is much more likely that the element in the early Church that maintained a concern for the outsider and the Gentile received its stimulus and guidance from the known example of Jesus in his own situation.

Again we can argue, since this attitude of Jesus to the outcast is established beyond any reasonable doubt, that the incidents recorded of particular cases of such friendship are *prima facie* historical, for instance, the story of the call of Levi at the customs office and the suggestion to Zacchaeus that Jesus should visit his house. This also would substantiate the genuineness of the words in which Jesus answered those who criticized him for such conduct, as for instance his retort: "The healthy do not need the doctor, but only the sick. I came not to seek the righteous but sinners."

Dodd and Jeremias have shown that a number of the parables of Jesus were originally spoken precisely to this situation, and as part of his answer to critics. Luke indeed states explicitly that the three parables included in Luke 15 were spoken as a reply to those who complained: "This man receives sinners and eats with them." That this understanding of some of the parables is correct we may accept as proved to the point of conclusiveness.

It was noted earlier that one of the features that is vouched for in all three primary sources is that Jesus gave missionary instructions to his disciples. The fact that instructions were given confirms the other evidence in the gospels for the fact of such a mission, and also for the fact that there were disciples to whom such instructions could be given. Since the word "disciple" means primarily a "learner," we may assume that they were men who received instruction from Jesus in order to prepare them for a future task. If so, we may say, in parenthesis, that the instructions they received and learned may well have provided some of the materials that were later remembered and recorded about Jesus and his teaching.

The fact that Jesus had "disciples" is confirmed by the fact that this name is not an Old Testament word at all. Nor is it one that could have come from the early Church, because so far as we can tell the word soon dropped out of use in the early Church. It does not occur at all in the epistles. So here, too, is a historical fact.

Similarly, in the gospels Jesus is frequently called "teacher" (or the Jewish equivalent, Rabbi). The word occurs no less than fifty times in the gospels. This, too, is something that could not have come from the early Church because they did not think of him as a teacher or use the word of him. The early Church applied titles of far loftier significance to Jesus.

Jesus, then, in his ministry was spoken of as a teacher. This may point to the reliability of the tradition, preserved in Mark 1:38 and 44, that he placed so much importance on teaching that he refused to let even the healing work take precedence over it.

Once again we may insist that this list of items does not exhaust the matter. It merely illustrates how one may proceed, and marks out some of the salient features in the gospels that may be accepted with confidence as historical.

There is another method by which one may begin to assemble items in the gospels that may be accepted as historical. It is not directly derived from the tests we have proposed, though indirectly it is. It is to note the conclusions of New Testament scholars who, on the basis of such tests as these, have wrestled with the problem and named those elements in the gospels which stand out for them as historical. From our point of view this is a practical rather than a theoretical approach, but it may well prove useful in indicating a basic nucleus from which we can start. We select some of the outstanding scholars in this field of research, who themselves, at one time if not now, felt compelled to adopt an extremely skeptical attitude toward the question of historicity in the gospels. We inquire from these scholars what items in the gospels they now feel compelled to accept as historical, in spite of their acute awareness of all the difficulties involved.

There is bound to be some overlapping in the items referred to, but it will be our aim to avoid repeating points, even though more than one scholar has emphasized them.

(1) We start with Bultmann, who has stated: "I do indeed think that we can now know almost nothing concerning the life and personality of Jesus." He does, however, concede the following few points as historically certain:[1]

(a) Jesus found himself vigorously opposed to the religious authorities of his time because of his defiance of their rigid interpretation of sabbath regulations. This would, however, have the effect of ascribing historical validity, in basic outline, to the recorded conflicts between Jesus and the Pharisees over this issue. If the conflict was in fact there, it is more likely that some of the precise disagreements would be remembered than that the later Church would have to invent specific cases to illustrate the existence of a conflict of which it knew only in broad outline.

(b) Jesus disregarded the rules of ritual purification as they were generally observed by strict Jews, as reported in Mark 7:3-4. If so, this would make it probable that Mark 7:1-23, especially verses 14-23, are substantially accurate.

(c) Jesus attacked the rigid legalism of the religious outlook of the Pharisees. They elevated their own rules to the status of laws of God. These then became rules that must not be broken or relaxed on any ground whatever, even if in some instances the rule became irrelevant and silly, or even unjust and callous. Instances of

---

[1] See, for instance, the excerpts from his writing in McArthur, *In Search of the Historical Jesus,* pp. 147-152, 161-163.

this are the pettifogging insistence on the tithing of such herbs as mint and cummin when they were brought in from the garden. This fastidious and useless practice they observed with punctiliousness, while neglecting such fundamentally important matters as mercy and justice (Matt. 23:23 and Luke 11:42). There is also the way oaths could be manipulated by those who knew the tricks of the trade, so as to defeat rather than uphold the expectation of honesty. An oath could be made binding or not according to what sacred authority you called on as you made your oath, as is clear from Matthew 23:16-22. The words of Jesus calling for the abandonment of all oath-taking as something that undermined rather than maintained common honesty, also reflect this sharp controversy (Matt. 5:34).

(d) Jesus showed sympathy for women and children, as reflected in the words attributed to him: "Suffer little children to come to me" (Mark 10:14) and "whoever offends one of these little ones..." (Mark 9:42). The prominence of women in the story of Jesus is most unexpected, and must be a genuine trait. Luke in particular feels that this feature should not be allowed to slip from notice, and prominence is given to such women as Mary and Martha of Bethany, the woman who was a sinner, Mary Magdalene, Mary the mother of Jesus, and others. This unusual degree of appreciation of both children and women is totally uncharacteristic of Judaism, and there is no evidence that it continued after the time of Jesus into the early Christian communities. At any rate, Paul, by common repute, was not an enthusiastic feminist!

(e) Jesus was not a strict ascetic of the type of John the Baptist, who, it is reported, was criticized by the Pharisees as a fanatic ("He has a demon," they said; Matt. 11:18 and Luke 7:33). The freer attitude of Jesus in this respect did not, however, win their approval, but rather their scornful indignation and hostility. They denounced him as "a gluttonous man and a winebibber." We may take it, therefore, as historical fact that Jesus did not observe the fasts prescribed by the Pharisees and accepted invitations to banquets in the homes of nonreligious people. This gives support to the authenticity of the reply of Jesus: "Can the wedding guests fast while the bridegroom is with them?" The early Church who later took up again the Jewish practice of regular fasting would not be likely to have invented this free and easy attitude of their founder toward fasting.

(2) In addition to these items named by Bultmann, we name two others that Kähler noted as bearing every mark of historicity, since they could not be derived either from contemporary Judaism or from early Christianity. Kähler's book *Der sogenannte historische Jesus und der geschichtliche biblische Christus* was written as far back as 1896, but Käsemann writes of it that "it is still hardly dated ... and has never been refuted" (*Essays on New Testament Themes*, p. 16).

(a) The first of these is the emphasis on "faith" found in the gospels. Jesus looked for it in those who came to him for help. We read such phrases as "seeing their faith," "your faith has healed you," "according to your faith be it done unto you." He shows impatience with those whose faith is qualified by an "if," "if thou wilt," "if thou canst." He rebuked his disciples with a word not found elsewhere in Greek literature (*oligopistoi*), usually translated into English by some such phrase as "O ye of little faith" or "How little faith you have" (NEB). He sighs: "If only you had faith like a mustard seed, you could move mountains."

In the synoptic gospels, however, "faith" means something very different from acceptance of a credal statement, such as belief in one God or in Jesus as the Son of God. It has nothing to do with creeds. It is a very simple attitude of believing that what Jesus is asked to do he (or God active in him) can and will do. When men brought to him faith like this, nothing was impossible. As Jesus said: "All things are possible to him who believes" (Mark 9:23), and "Whoever says to this mountain, 'Be taken up and cast into the sea,' and does not doubt in his heart, but believes that what he says will come to pass, it will be done for him" (Mark 11:23).

The understanding of faith in this particular sense is not characteristic of the meaning of faith as found either in Judaism or early Christianity, and Kähler strongly argues that it must be a historical feature.

(b) Kähler also notes that Jesus' offer of God's unconditional forgiveness is quite different from the standard teaching of Judaism, which offered forgiveness only on evidence of real penitence; otherwise forgiveness was felt to offer encouragement to moral carelessness. The early Christians also seem to have shared something of this same apprehension about moral standards, and instituted penances to safeguard them. Hence the dangerous freedom with which Jesus offered forgiveness is not likely to have been an invention. He is recorded as saying to a paralyzed youth: "Your sins are forgiven." Of the woman who wept at his feet, he said: "Her sins, many as they are, are forgiven." In the parable in Matthew 18 the master "had pity on" the insolvent servant and "forgave him the debt"; and later when the servant acted callously toward a defaulting fellow servant he reminds him: "I forgave you all that debt.... Should not you have had mercy?" God's forgiveness is offered freely to man, but it is expected that it will produce in the forgiven man a forgiving attitude to those who have wronged him.

(3) Probably of all Bultmann's disciples Bornkamm is the one who has particularly found himself compelled by his further studies to acknowledge as historical many features that appear in the gospels. His book *Jesus of Nazareth* is a most important one, both for this particular issue of historicity and also for the proper appreciation of the total significance of Jesus. Chapter III in his book is of special importance for our present consideration.

(a) Bornkamm finds himself greatly impressed by the convincing character of the people who come into the story of Jesus—priest and scribe, Pharisee and publican, rich and poor, healthy and sick, righteous and sinner. He writes: "They appear in the story in a matter-of-fact and simple fashion, chosen at random and appearing in no particular order. Yet all the characters, however great their diversity, present a very human appearance. In their encounter with Jesus, they come as *fully real people*."

(b) Second, he gives his judgment that it should be recognized as a genuine characteristic of Jesus that he can sense what is going on in the minds of those who confront him. He speaks of Jesus' "perception and penetrating insight." This is "a most characteristic trait of the historical Jesus." The incidents where this characteristic is shown are those concerning the rich young ruler, Zacchaeus, Jairus, James and John, the woman with the hemorrhage, the Pharisees who came to test him, etc.

(c) He believes also that the authority of Jesus in the gospels is a real and not an invented characteristic. "He speaks as one with authority and not as the scribes," is the recorded comment. Jesus gives the impression of possessing a right to speak directly about God and God's will. He does not appeal to past authorities. What he says sounds true. Bornkamm calls this an "essential feature of the historical Jesus." He speaks of it as "his astonishing sovereignty," as he sees through his opponents' prevarications and by shrewdly directed questions forces them to answer their own objections. We have already noted the frequency of the question in the reported words of Jesus, and should agree with Bornkamm that this must surely be a historical feature. Such questions were: "Who proved himself neighbor? How think ye? Which of them will love him most?", etc.

Bornkamm finds the same unmistakable authority in the dealings of Jesus with those who came to him for help. There is no hint of any inability to cope with the problem presented. He is the strong man entering the house, to dispossess the usurper who has occupied it. "He steps into the battlefield between God and Satan's power."

So, too, in his dealings with his disciples—he calls them and he rebukes them (speaking of them all as "men of little faith" and of one of them as "Satan"). He sends them out on dangerous and ill-provided mission journeys. He is able to hold their loyalty even when his general popularity begins to wane, and the danger and cost of continued discipleship has become unmistakably clear.

This authority, Bornkamm insists, is "a reality which appertains to the historical Jesus and is prior to any interpretation."

(d) A further point that Bornkamm makes is that there is an "essential mystery about Jesus," and part of this is that he is able "to make the reality of God present." This characteristic in fact dominates all the gospels, and Bornkamm is convinced that it cannot be other than an authentic memory. Jesus appeared as one who proclaimed the nearness of the rule of God (that is, the nearness of God as he takes charge of human life). This rule (Kingdom) is not a distant hope, but a present reality. It is already dawning and demands instant decision.

Many of the parables of Jesus reflect this urgent situation, and summon men to resolute decision because God confronts them. Such parables as the Thief in the Night and the Ten Virgins, although in Matthew they are associated with the expectation of the second coming of Christ, probably in their historical setting referred to this immediate or imminent confrontation with God.

The words of Jesus also present God as present in the normal, everyday life of the world, although men are largely unaware of what is taking place. But, in fact, not even a sparrow falls without the Father's knowledge.

This message of the Kingdom and the presence of God in his care and command in all life's situations is not, argues Bornkamm, characteristic of either Judaism or early Christianity, and so must be treated, as it occurs in the gospels, as authentic.

(e) There is also the constant insistence in the gospels on the complete seriousness of God's will for man. This will, as revealed for instance in the beatitudes, is no invention—his commendation of the poor, the mourners, the humble, those "who cannot live without righteousness" (they hunger and thirst for it), the merciful, the peacemaker, the persecuted. Nor can we regard as "invented" his insistence that God's will requires purity of heart, utter truthfulness, and a readiness for a love that no longer knows of either retaliation or exclusion of the enemy.

(4) Käsemann has already been quoted as insisting that there are pieces of the synoptic tradition "which the historian must acknowledge as authentic." He would not dissent from many of the points already noted as authentic by other authors. Two items, however, not already precisely named, he includes in those which could not have been invented:

(a) The authenticity of some of the "antitheses" in the Sermon on the Mount, especially the first, second, and fourth, that is, those which forbid anger (resentment) as well as murder, lustful thinking as well as an adulterous act, any misleading statement as well as formal oath-breaking.

(b) Jesus' expectation of love for neighbor, which is directed by intelligent understanding and spontaneous personal decision rather than merely blind obedience to an imposed authority, must also be authentic. Jesus throws back responsibility for decision in a moral issue upon the conscience of the individual: "How think ye?" "Judge ye yourselves what is right." "Is it lawful on the sabbath to do good or to do harm, to save life or to kill?" He does not seek to override a person's own sense of what is right, but rather to awaken and guide it.

All these "uninventable" characteristics of Jesus, as named above, are now conceded by scholars who at one time had been inclined to abandon the possibility of gaining any historical knowledge of Jesus. For this reason these elements, now granted to be historical as the result of a change of mind, carry a certain extra persuasiveness, since they have been acknowledged only under the constraint of unexpectedly compelling reasons.

Other scholars such as Vincent Taylor, T. W. Manson, C. H. Dodd, and J. Jeremias, all experts of the highest eminence in New Testament scholarship, would probably allow as firmly historical a much larger list of features

than those just named, though Dodd in his recent book
The Founder of Christianity, in the chapter entitled "Personal Traits," is content to confine himself in the main
to those which have been already noted, such as the
authority of Jesus (though "an authority which respected
the freedom of the person"), his sympathy with those
"who labored under a disabling sense of guilt," his power
to inspire those who came to him with "new confidence,"
that is, "faith," and his method of "leading the questioner
to answer his own questions."

We may therefore, without undue credulity, accept the
cautious judgments recorded in this chapter as offering
a solid nucleus of authentic material, and we may sum-
marize it as follows:

Jesus came from Nazareth in Galilee, and spoke Ara-
maic as his native tongue. His parents were known as
Joseph and Mary. He had four brothers and some sisters
He earned his living at Nazareth as a carpenter.

His public work began when he identified himself with
the prophet known as John the Baptist, and accepted baptism at his hands. He died by crucifixion, executed by
the Roman authorities in Palestine as one suspected of
threatening danger to the Roman rule and security.

His public activity was characterized by teaching and
healing. As a teacher people noted his authority. This
same authority was evidenced in his competence in the
presence of illness, his power to command and retain the
loyalty of his closest followers, his ability to confront in-
fluential and powerful opponents with complete effec-
tiveness.

He had remarkable gifts for healing people's illnesses.
He freely offered God's forgiveness. He asked from those
who came in their need a response in "faith," a confidence
that God could and would take effective action through
him.

He especially reached out to those who were treated
as outcasts of society by the religious leaders, offering
them friendship and gladly responding to their gestures

of friendship, even to the point of accepting their hospitality. He did not hesitate to acknowledge his deep concern for both women and little children, and his happiness in their company.

From among his followers he brought a small, chosen number into a specially close relationship with him of committed discipleship. He trained them for their later tasks and in due course entrusted them with a share in his mission.

He gave great offense to the religious leaders of the time. This was caused in part by what he did in freely associating with disreputable people, and, so far from leading the ascetic life of John the Baptist, gladly accepting their invitations to share in their meals. Sometimes also he challenged and defied the commonly accepted standards of behavior that were observed by the religious leaders and which they regarded as representing a true obedience to God. He would not, for instance, submit to their rigid sabbath regulations nor to their various rules about clean and unclean foods and ritual purifications. He disputed their legalistic views of God and morality.

All the people who came into the story—his enemies, his friends, and those who came to ask his help—appear as real people, and in his relationship with all of them Jesus shows an unusual power of perception into their characters and motives.

His message as a teacher was about God and God's rule in human life. He made the nearness of God very real to others. He spoke as one who knew that God is always seeking entry into human life and constantly at work, unseen and unsuspected, in the world of nature. He spoke about God's will, but in a very different way from the conventional piety of current religious teaching. What God asks of men is portrayed in the strange standards of goodness embodied in the beatitudes. He insisted that obedience to God is far more than an outward avoidance of murder, adultery, and the breaking of oaths. It reaches also into men's inner thoughts and feelings,

calling them to abandon all resentment, all lustful im-
agining, all deceit. He asked from men a love for others
that acknowledges no limitations of any kind, a love that
is offered even toward enemies and strangers and those
who do us wrong, and a spirit of forgiveness that never
gives up. The obedience to God for which he calls is not,
however, an unreasoning submission to external authority
but an intelligent insight into the rightness of what God
asks, and a voluntary acceptance of it by one's own free
choice.

This solid and fairly extensive nucleus of historical certainty makes a reasonably encouraging start.

Chapter 8

Historical Facts in the Ministry of Jesus

The Tradition That Peter Was One of Mark's Sources of Information

Mark is the earliest of our four gospels, and itself a source used by both Matthew and Luke. Because of its earliness it has usually in recent years been thought to be the gospel least affected by theological interpretations. Being closest in time to the events he records, it is argued that probably Mark reported them most accurately. Moreover, there is a very early tradition that closely associated Mark's gospel with the preaching of Peter the apostle. If there were truth in this, the probability of a strong historical element in Mark would be greatly enhanced. There has, however, in recent years been a determination to trace back all the gospel materials to units derived from the life of the Christian communities. The preoccupation with this assumption has meant that the tradition that Mark owed some of his stories and sequences to the eyewitness memories of Peter has been largely discounted and ignored. Nineham at one point seems to concede that there is some truth in it, writing: "It may well be that some of the material in the gospel does derive ultimately from Peter" (p. 51). But a little later he abandons the possibility: "Most contemporary scholars agree that in places St. Mark's material bears all the signs of having been community tradition and cannot therefore be derived directly from St. Peter or any other eyewitness. But once that admission has been made about some of Mark's material, it seems only logical to go on and make it about *all* his material." This seems a very odd statement. Why should it be "logical" to apply to the whole of Mark what is found to be probably true of Mark only *in places?* It is indeed at those points where the material in Mark does not seem to be the product of community influences that we find ourselves wondering if some of the stories may not come ultimately from an eyewitness.

Since the link between Peter and Mark has been dismissed in a somewhat offhand manner by many recent writers, and since its importance is obvious for anyone inquiring about historicity in Mark, it seems appropriate to take another look at the subject.

The oldest authority for this link between Mark and Peter is a paragraph from an early writer called Papias. He was Bishop of Hierapolis in Asia Minor in the early days of the second century. He tells us that he made it his business to make inquiries from any Christian of a previous generation whom he met and to record what he had to say in a book. This actual book has been lost and only a few quotations from it are known, as they happen to appear in the writings of later authors. Eusebius, the church historian at the beginning of the fourth century, quotes from Papias' book at some length. One quotation recalls a statement by someone called "the elder": "The elder used to say this also: Mark indeed, who became the interpreter of Peter, wrote accurately as far as he remembered them, the things said and done by the Lord, but not however in order. For he had neither heard the Lord nor been his personal follower, but at a later stage, as I said, he had followed Peter, who used to adapt his teachings to the needs (of his hearers), but not as though he were drawing up a connected account of the oracles of the Lord. So then Mark made no mistake in thus recording some things just as he remembered them."

E. Schweizer in his 1971 commentary *The Good News according to Mark* (p. 25) agrees with Nineham in dismissing this tradition from Papias as unacceptable. He does, however, do what other scholars do not trouble to do, and very commendably pauses to give the grounds for his rejection. He lists three: (1) "It is very unlikely that Peter carried on missionary work with the help of an interpreter." (2) "The expression 'memories' [the word Papias uses of them] is fitting neither for Peter's preaching nor for Mark's book." (3) "The primary objection is that there is no evidence of any particular Petrine tradition in Mark."

None of these three objections is at all convincing.

Concerning (1), it seems more than probable that a Galilean fisherman would need help in communicating with people if he went as a missionary in Greek-speaking areas. Concerning (2), we would claim that there are several vivid and detailed narratives in Mark, which for some reason he felt unable to curtail, and these stories do in fact read very much as if they were "memories"—such stories as those about "Legion," the woman with the hemorrhage, Jairus' daughter, and the epileptic boy. (3) seems particularly strange. As we hope to show later, there is much in Mark that finds a ready explanation if Peter can be taken as the authority behind it—e.g., the disparaging remarks about the disciples collectively and the uncomplimentary portrayal of Peter himself.

It is illuminating to be given by Schweizer his grounds for rejecting this Petrine tradition, because most scholars brush it aside without bothering to give reasons. But if the three arguments he proposes are the strongest available, their very frailty suggests that it is time we looked again at the tradition and asked whether there might not be stronger arguments for respecting it than those given for rejecting it.[1]

This belief in a link between Mark and Peter is not just an isolated piece of gossip connected with the single name of Papias. It is frequently affirmed in the years following him. In the second century, for instance, it reappears in the so-called Marcionite prologues to the gospels, and in the writings of Justin Martyr and of Irenaeus; and in the third century in Clement of Alexandria and Origen. These represent the responsible leadership of the Church in widely different areas of the Church's life. It means that the tradition was known and accepted over a wide area.

The mere acceptance of a tradition, however, does not make it true. We no longer take at face value the tradition that the first and fourth gospels were actually written by original disciples of Jesus. Where a tradition clearly bolsters up the official Church policy of the time and is used by the Church to provide authority for an official line that it is adopting, we may be justified in being suspicious. We should feel suspicious about the link between Peter and Mark, if there was any evidence that the developing Church sponsored it deliberately in order to uphold the authority of either Peter or Mark's gospel. This, however, does not at all appear to be the case. Mark is the gospel that portrays Peter in the least heroic guise. It is Matthew that removes many of Mark's crude references to Peter and introduces those passages on which his authority in the Church has been built. It is in Matthew that Peter is called the Rock on which the Church is built, the one to whom the keys of the Kingdom are given. Papias' tradition does nothing to enhance the reputation of Peter. Moreover, as compared with Matthew, in the life of the Church Mark is totally overshadowed by the more comprehensive and balanced gospel that preceded it, not only in the established sequence but also

---

[1] Jeremias in his book *New Testament Theology, Vol. I: The Proclamation of Jesus* gives strong support for this tradition about Peter and Mark and on pp. 90-91 gives some of the reasons for his opinion.

in both official and popular standing. So second rate
was Mark regarded by the official attitude of the Church
that it came to be accepted that his shorter gospel was
a somewhat pointless abbreviation of Matthew, with therefore no independent value of its own. Not only, therefore, was Peter's reputation not enhanced by any supposed
link with Mark's gospel, but Peter's supposed link with
Mark was not allowed to enhance the significance of Mark
as against the officially sponsored Matthew.

The tradition therefore of Peter's link with Mark appears to be one that served no official purpose whatever.
It survived, not to serve some important Church policy
but in spite of its divergence from such a policy. Should
not this fact make us pause and ask if therefore the tradition might not be true? Did it not survive for the sole
reason that it was known to be true, even though it
served no ecclesiastical purpose? Clearly the tradition
was something of an embarrassment to the Church. How
was it possible to establish the claim that Matthew was
the first gospel to be written, if it was also true that
Mark reproduced Peter's eyewitness stories? It is the
very fact that the tradition is one that the Church did
not use, one indeed that the Church found it very difficult to accommodate, which makes one think there may
very well be some inescapable truth behind it. A tradition that came into being and survived in spite of its
divergence from official policy is one that merits more
careful scrutiny than one that proved a welcome convenience in supporting the later policies of the Church.

Features in Mark That Favor a Link with Peter

There are in Mark several stories told with a wealth
of detail, often detail that is quite irrelevant to any perma-
nent spiritual value the story may have, indeed just the
kind that, as Nineham agrees, we "associate with an eyewitness." Usually stories in the gospels survived only as

"streamlined versions" as they were continually repeated in the life of the community by those who had no personal link with Jesus and no firsthand knowledge of his ministry. Unnecessary details in this process came to be excluded and only items relevant to the main thrust of the narrative as an instrument of the kerygma were retained. Some of these "streamlined" versions are to be found in Mark, for instance, in the Pronouncement Stories of Mark 2:15-3:6. But there are also these other stories which have not been trimmed down to a bare minimum, which Nineham agrees we usually associate with eyewitnesses. Such stories include the narratives about Legion, Jairus' daughter, the epileptic boy, etc.

In dealing with possible historical features in the gospels we found a certain impressiveness about those features which came to be acknowledged as historical by scholars who at first had discounted their historicity. The same approach may be followed here. Perhaps the first and most radical of British Form Critics, one who expounded the radical position of Bultmann for British readers, was R. H. Lightfoot. In his earlier books he had argued that the materials in the gospels did not allow us to claim historical knowledge of Jesus. He discounted the tradition of Peter's link with Mark. Later, however, in his *Gospel Message of St. Mark* he found himself obliged to concede that some passages in Mark now seemed to him to have all the appearance of being Petrine memories. There were three passages that he assigned to this category: Mark 1:16-39, a section that appears to retain a remembered chronological sequence—the call of four disciples, the visit to the synagogues with the healing of the man possessed by a demon, followed by the visit to Peter's home and the healing of his mother-in-law; Mark 5:21-43: the interwoven stories of the coming of Jairus to Jesus for help, the interruption and delay caused by the importunity of the woman with the hemorrhage and her healing, and finally the healing of Jairus' little daughter, regarded as dead; and Mark 9:2-29: the story of the Transfiguration of Jesus, followed by the healing of the epileptic boy.

It is significant that these stories are vivid and detailed as eyewitness stories might well be, and not the kind that have been molded and condensed until nothing but the bare essentials are left. They do not appear in the forms characteristic of units shaped by communities.

Vincent Taylor in his well-known commentary on Mark takes very seriously the early tradition about Peter and Mark, and is convinced that even more material in Mark than Lightfoot allows could well be explained as Mark's own telling of stories first heard from Peter. Taylor speaks of Papias' words as "the invaluable Papias tradition." He adds: "If we did not possess it, we should be compelled to postulate something very much like it," so strongly was he impressed by elements in Mark that, he felt, could best be explained as coming from an eyewitness. He fully concurred in accepting the three passages ascribed to the Petrine tradition by Lightfoot, but added four others also. These were Mark 4:35-5:20: the storm on the lake and the vivid story of the healing of "Legion"; Mark 6:30-56: the feeding of the five thousand and the story of Jesus coming to his disciples over the water; Mark 7:24-37: the story of the healing of the daughter of the Syro-phoenician woman on Gentile territory and the healing of the man who was deaf with the help of the shouted word "Ephphatha"; and Mark 8:27-9:1: the confession of Peter at Caesarea Philippi.

There are therefore good preliminary grounds for showing special regard for this Papias tradition linking Mark with Peter. First, it has strong ancient support, even though it is quite at variance with the official position adopted by the developing Church. Second, scholars of the highest repute have found in it the best available explanation of some vivid eyewitness narratives that Mark includes in his gospel. We will now look more closely at some of the features of these narratives and of the gospel as a whole which have made scholars postulate Mark's reliance on an eyewitness.

First there is the racy vividness of some of the narratives, so full of lifelike details. In explanation of these details we have to say either that Mark retained them because he had the stories in that form from someone whose memory he trusted, or else Mark was a wonderfully skilled novelist who could take a small incident coming to him in the rounded, contracted form of a community tradition and for some reason of his own embellish it with lifelike details in order to make the story sound more realistic and exciting. I personally find it very difficult to believe that Mark was this kind of fiction writer. My impression is that he wrote what he had every reason to believe had actually happened as he told it.

All these "lifelike details" are found, not in the stories told in the "rounded" forms attributable to community molding, but in the long, expansive narratives that both Matthew and Luke, when they took them over, felt compelled to reduce in length, and did so by omitting these very details. It is just these longer stories which Lightfoot and Taylor felt might well come from an eyewitness.

The kind of details that either come from the memory of one who was present, or else are highly skillful fictions created for the sake of verisimilitude, are as follows:

Mark 1:20: "James and John left their father Zebedee in the boat with the hired servants." There seems to be no possible theological reason for introducing father Zebedee and the hired servants. It is arguable that the mention of Zebedee and the boat is introduced to stress the truth that "following Jesus" "may involve the severance of family and personal ties" (so Nineham). But Nineham finds great difficulty in the "hired servants." He merely asks, without answering the question: "Does the reference serve to defend the apostles against the charge of abandoning their aged father, or does it add pathos—he is now left entirely at the mercy of 'hirelings.' "

Mark 4:38: "Teacher, do you not care if we perish?" is the cry of the frightened disciples in the threatened boat, while Jesus sleeps "in the stern on a cushion." Are these details fictional—Jesus sleeping, the mention of the "cushion," the sharp discourtesy of the disciples' words? Would theological motives have worked out these details for some didactic purpose? We noticed that Matthew, so far from finding valuable theological material in the details, had to modify the agitated cry of the disciples. It all leaves the impression of an accurate actual memory.

Mark 5:2-15: The story about "Legion" is told with a wealth of detail, and it makes an enthralling narrative. One would not wish for one detail fewer. Matthew, however, who wants only what contributes significantly to the essential meaning of the episode, reduces Mark's narrative to less than half its original proportions by leaving out much of the unnecessary detail. His omissions include Mark's detailed description of the sick and violent man: "He lived among the tombs; and no one could bind him any more, even with a chain; for he had often been bound with fetters and chains, but the chains he wrenched apart and the fetters he broke in pieces; and no one had strength to subdue him." This could well be understood as the comment of one who was present and knew the local gossip about the extremity of the man's insanity. They are much less understandable as purely fictional creations. At the end of the story Mark adds the comment that the people of the area "began to plead with Jesus to leave their district." This, too, seems like the recollection of a very surprising request, rather than as a subtle invention with some obscure theological significance.

Mark 5:30: When the ailing woman touched Jesus from behind in the crowd, Jesus stopped and asked: "Who touched me?" The disciples were sarcastic in their reply that dozens of people must in fact have touched him as they pressed around to get near him. This reads like a real situation rather than an invented one with a theological purpose. Later we read that Jesus "did not allow anyone to accompany him [into the little girl's sickroom at Jairus' house] except Peter, James and John." This, too, reads like a memory. James and John appear to have played no great part in the early Church after the death of Jesus. Their association with Peter at this stage is more likely to be a recollection than a later invention

to explain how they came to be associated with Peter in
the growing hierarchy of the Church.

Mark 7:24-37: This is the remarkable story about Jesus
and the Syrophoenician woman. It is incredible to think
that this is an invented story. There is so much in it that
is puzzling, if not actually offensive. It is hard to associate some of the details with what believers later came
to attribute to Jesus. No wonder Luke discreetly leaves
it out. As an invention of the later Church, what would
it be meant to teach? The exclusion of Gentiles from the
mission of the Church? But Jesus did eventually help
this Gentile woman's daughter. Is it therefore meant to
provide authority for the Gentile mission of the Church?
But Jesus acts so grudgingly that it is a very doubtful
authority that the story confers. Surely the best explanation is that the story is told as Mark had heard it told
by an eyewitness.

From the longer narratives in Mark points like these
can be multiplied. If one has made a prior decision that
all his material must have come from the community
teaching of the Church, then some explanation other than
historicity has to be found. But if one is not bound to
such a prior decision, these elements have all the sound
of authenticity.

If there are, then, elements in Mark's gospel that have
all the character of eyewitness recollections, who was the
eyewitness? The oldest tradition said "Peter," though we
may be quite sure that the tradition arose on quite other
grounds than a need to account for these vivid details in
the gospel.

Tradition and some of Mark's vivid, lifelike stories therefore may be said to provide confirmation of each other.

A second ground for thinking that Peter might lie behind Mark's narratives is the derogatory way Mark speaks
about Peter and the other disciples. This occurs so re-
peatedly that one scholar has said: "Mark hates the twelve."
Certainly he includes many disparaging references to them:
"Why are you such cowards?" (NEB) says Jesus to them at
Mark 4:40. In 8:17 he says to them: "Do you not yet

perceive? Are your hearts hardened?" In 14:40 we read:
"Jesus came again and found them sleeping, for their eyes
were heavy; and they did not know what to answer him."
At 9:33-34 the disciples are rebuked for their selfish place-
seeking, when they are caught arguing about which of
them is most entitled to a position of special privilege. At
Mark 10:35 James and John, bent on their own selfish
advancement at the expense of their colleagues, try to
persuade Jesus to promise them the places of highest status.
At Mark 10:32 Jesus is shown walking on ahead and the
disciples dragging along behind, "amazed and afraid."

Peter is included with the others in these rebukes of
Jesus and, in addition, is portrayed personally on a number of occasions as acting or speaking foolishly, and in
such a way as himself to incur severe reprimands. At
Mark 9:6 on the Mount of Transfiguration he blurts out
a silly suggestion about which Mark comments: "He did
not know what to say; they were so terrified" (NEB). At
Caesarea Philippi, after his confession of Jesus as "Christ,"
Peter presumes to rebuke Jesus for speaking words that
anticipate coming suffering and death and receives a very
sharp censure in return: "Away with you, Satan; you think
as men think, not as God thinks." In the story of the Passion, Peter's boastful assurances of unfaltering loyalty are
emphasized, and with them Jesus' warnings of his coming failures. On one occasion when the disciples sleep
in Gethsemane it is to Peter personally that Jesus says:
"Simon, could you not stay awake one hour?" His threefold denial of Jesus is told in harrowing detail; and after
it all "he broke down and wept." After that he does not
appear again in the story, except that the women at the
empty tomb are told to make sure that Peter knows
about it.

It seems strange that the disciples, who were soon to
be revered in the Church as the founding apostles, and
Peter, who became chief among them as the Church developed, should be shown in such a poor light. It is incredible that the later Church should invent these stories
and ascribe such words to Jesus. The thinking of the

later Church on these matters is reflected rather in the known way in which Matthew softens or removes these offensive passages. How then can these words be explained? Is it not most likely that they represent what actually happened and are recorded because they were known to have happened? If this is so, who would tell the stories in a way so disparaging toward the disciples as a whole and to Peter in particular? Is there any better suggestion than that Peter himself so told the stories? Looking back in the light of his later faith and in utter shame at his own weakness and unreliability under pressure, he might well have told them just like this. Certainly it is easier to think that it was one of the disciples who spoke in this way than that it was a later Christian. If it was one of the disciples, it is easier to think that it was Peter who spoke so slightingly about himself than that another disciple so underlined his weaknesses.

A third consideration that may support Peter's link with Mark's gospel is the use in Mark of Aramaic words when recording sayings of Jesus. At Mark 3:28 we meet what seems to have been a characteristic mannerism used by Jesus to introduce an important affirmation. He starts with the Aramaic word "Amen." This is not made clear in English translations, which usually represent it by "truly." But it is in fact an Aramaic and not a Greek word that is being translated. This mannerism of Jesus is represented in all the other three gospels as well. Most scholars would regard it as a characteristic of Jesus' mode of speech, which was so well remembered that all the different traditions included it. Its presence in Mark's gospel does not of itself prove more than this. But there are other Aramaic words in Mark that the other evangelists do not reproduce, because they were single instances and not recurring forms of speech. There are, for instance, the words "Talitha Cumi" (Mark 5:41) by which Jesus roused Jairus' daughter from her deathlike sleep. Mark also adds the meaning of the words in Greek, as well as recording the actual words spoken by Jesus in Aramaic. Why, then, did he bother to include the Aramaic words at all? Very few of his readers would understand them. It may have some significance that Peter is reported to have been one of the three disciples present when this happened. Unless we have some deep conviction on other grounds that eye-witness evidence is totally impossible, quite the simplest explanation is that these words of Jesus produced such an astonishing result that they remained embedded in the memory of one of the bystanders, and afterwards when he told the story he found himself repeating the sound of the very words Jesus had spoken, even though he had afterwards to translate them into Greek for the benefit of his non-Aramaic hearers.

Similarly, we could explain the other Aramaic word "Ephphatha" in Mark 7:34. Again there is no need whatever for Mark to retain the Aramaic, for he immediately gives its meaning in Greek. The other evangelists do not keep the Aramaic, since it serves no useful purpose. The story is about the cure by Jesus of a man who is deaf and who would therefore be unable to hear when Jesus spoke in an ordinary tone of voice. So Jesus uses visual methods of awakening his expectancy and confidence. He touches his ears and places saliva on his tongue, since he suffered also from an impediment of speech. Jesus would have to shout the words of healing so that the deaf man might hear something of what was said. Again it would seem a not unreasonable explanation to suggest that the cure left such a vivid memory with Peter that the unforgettable Aramaic word shouted by Jesus was given a place in the story whenever he told it.

If this sounds at all fanciful, it is less fanciful than the only alternative that has been suggested. This is that in the healing practice of the early Church it was customary to believe that some healing formula spoken in a foreign tongue had specially effective magical powers, and that these stories therefore deliberately provided certain mysterious words that recognized healers might use in the healing work of the post-resurrection Church. So far as I know, there is not the slightest evidence that such foreign words of supposed magical power were in fact used by the early Christians in their healing ministries. Even if anyone did use either "Talitha Cumi" or "Ephphatha," it would be because they occurred in the gospel records, and not the other way around, that they were read back into the gospel records because they were in common use in the later Church. But were they in common use? If this were in fact the explanation, why did Matthew omit them? He represents the later Church far more than Mark does, and if foreign words of magical significance were needed, he would have been more likely to introduce them than to omit them in his editing of Mark.

There is also the prayer of Jesus in Gethsemane that Mark records as addressed to "Abba, Father" (Mark 14:36), giving both the Aramaic word that Jesus used and its nearest Greek equivalent. Matthew dispenses with the Aramaic word and retains only the Greek one. We know that this Aramaic word "Abba" survived as a privileged form of address to God used by Christians who had been brought into a new relationship with him through Christ. It expressed their joyous awareness that they were sons of God their Father. Paul's letters show that it came to be used by Christians in the Greek world who would be totally unfamiliar with the Aramaic language (see Rom. 8:15 and Gal. 4:6). It is incredible that it should have arisen in Greek Christianity and been read back into the gospels. Its presence in Greek Christianity must mean that it was remembered that this word embodied a recollection of Jesus' practice. Its presence in Mark could be explained as a recollection of Peter that this was the characteristic way in which Jesus prayed.

One is not unaware of the intricate and complicated explanations of Mark's gospel that have been suggested by Austin Farrer, Bishop Carrington and W. Marxsen, all of which if accepted would tell against the use of a Petrine source by Mark. One can only say that the presence of Petrine recollections in Mark seems to us less improbable than the other theories (without base in tradition) that make Mark into a man of extremely subtle, even tortuous, mental processes, and which, to my mind, totally misrepresent him.

If then there is material that came to Mark from the preaching of Peter, as he related incidents that had impressed themselves unforgettably on his mind during his time with Jesus, then these materials have the highest claim to historicity.

Historical Facts from the Ministry of Jesus

In a previous chapter we tried to assemble those features and characteristics of the personality of Jesus which come through to us from the pages of the gospels, which have every claim to be regarded as historical. We must now try to discover what *events* can be established as historical, and the sequence in which they occurred.

It is agreed that the materials in the gospels do not provide the evidence from which a full-scale biography can be written. Many of the incidents and sayings are not placed in any kind of historical sequence. One clearly established conclusion of Form Criticism is that in the main the materials now in the gospels circulated for a time, during the oral period, as isolated items. There was no recollection preserved either of their precise context in the ministry of Jesus or of their chronological relationship to other items. Whether an incident happened before or after another did not appear important. It was its spiritual or theological significance that mattered. Moreover, in the main only those events were recorded about Jesus which seemed important in the propagation of the Gospel. So we look in vain either for any ordered chronological account of various episodes, or for such information as would be of great historical interest to us but valueless for faith, such as the color of Jesus' hair and eyes, whether he was tall or short, casual or particular in his dress. We do not know the length of his ministry, or how old he was when it started, or his age when he died. These limitations must be accepted.

Even though a chronological biography cannot be written, that does not mean, however, that a reliable historical portrait may not be recoverable. Indeed, we have already seen that much can be regarded as authentic—the impression he made on others, the way people reacted to him, his influence over people, and the attitudes they adopted to him. The substance of his teaching can in part be determined and some characteristics of his teaching method and style.

The lack of sequence and continuity in Mark's narrative can, however, be exaggerated. We are not wholly without some clear indications of a developing pattern. There is, for instance, no doubt that at the end of Jesus' life stands the cross, and it is usually believed that the earliest continuous piece of narrative to be written or told was the story of the passion. Once this story was told, it would have to be pushed further and further back. Perhaps at first it would describe only the execution itself. But then the question would be asked why Jesus was executed by the Romans, since only they could use the cross as the means of execution, and since even by the Romans it was restricted to the execution of dangerous rebels. Then the question would arise how he came to fall into the hands of the Romans when the chief conflict had been with the Jewish leaders. And how did they get him into their power? So the episodes of Judas and the trial before the high priest would be brought into the story. Each new stage introduced would require an earlier one to explain it. Some explanation was needed to account for the hostility of the religious leaders to Jesus and the circumstances that led to Jesus' presence in Jerusalem at that particular Passover.

It is probable that Mark had told his story verbally—perhaps dozens of times—before it took its final form in the written gospel. We may not be able to vouch for the accuracy of every step in the story, but the sequence of events immediately leading up to the death of Jesus has the right to be regarded as fairly near to history. If Mark himself told the story as he remembered Peter to have told it, then the probability of a considerable degree of accuracy is increased.

My own personal impression is that Mark intended to write what he believed to be factually true. Undoubtedly he believed that Jesus was the Son of God, and wished his writings to bring people to that same belief. But he believed that it was Jesus as he was who was the Son of God. He did not feel the need to bowdlerize and purge the actual story to make it consistent with preconceived notions of what the Son of God ought to be like. He makes no attempt, for instance, to make Jesus himself claim to be the Christ. James Barr comments on this absence of the tendency to heighten the tradition (*Scottish Journal of Theology*, 1955, p. 229): "We see here the richness of that consciousness of the early Church in which one like Mark could believe in Jesus as the Son of God and yet could record and transmit with fidelity a tradition in which Jesus never so spoke."

That is the impression that Mark the evangelist leaves on me personally, the impression of one who is content to record the facts as he understood them because they were facts about Jesus. He has no interest in later human attempts to improve on these facts, which in themselves made him worthy to be acknowledged as the Son of God.

Even in Mark, however, there is much that makes no claim to be chronological. Quite early in the story Mark indicates that signs of hostility to Jesus from the religious leaders had already begun to appear. In 2:1-3:6 are grouped five so-called "conflict stories." No doubt Mark, by putting them early in the story, intended readers to understand that this hostility began to appear very early in the course of Jesus' ministry. But it would be misleading to argue that these five incidents all took place in quick succession. They probably happened at widely separate intervals. Mark puts them together because they serve to illustrate the hostility that was the seedbed out of which the determination to destroy Jesus grew. The arrangement is topical, not chronological.

The same is true of the parables and other sayings of

Jesus. Mark groups several parables together in chapter 4, not to make us think that they were all spoken at the same time, but because he is giving illustrations of this characteristic mode of his teaching. The parables would be spoken on quite separate occasions at which we can now only guess. Similarly, we cannot place the healings in any sequence, nor can we say whether any individual episode came early or late in the story.

The same is true of the recorded *events*. Mark by an indirect hint gives a clear indication that the feeding of the five thousand took place about the time of the Passover, since he mentions that the grass was green. But we do not know whether it was one, two, three, or four Passovers before the one on which he died. Similarly, such incidents as his welcome to the children, the quarreling of the disciples, the inquiry of the rich young ruler, and the ambitious request of James and John cannot be placed in any kind of relative sequence or assigned to any place either early or late in the ministry. Nor does it seem to matter at all that we lack this kind of information. Historicity of this kind is unimportant.

It is, however, grossly overstating the case to say that in Mark there is no developing pattern at all. Mark's gospel is clearly based on an accepted outline of the main events in the ministry of Jesus, into which other material has been introduced largely on a topical basis. Some scholars claim that even this minimal outline is Mark's own invention, that he had no real knowledge of any sequence at all but simply used his ingenuity to think one up. Again we remind ourselves that only thirty years separated the writing of Mark from the events he records. Over such a short period crucial events are certainly remembered and also the relative order in which they occurred. For instance, the interval between 1973 and the 1939-1945 war is approximately the same interval as that between the ministry of Jesus and Mark's writing of his gospel. For one who was an adult during that war the main events still stand out in their historical sequence— Dunkirk, the Americans' entry into the war, Alamein, D

Day, VE Day, and VJ Day. But the other events, some of them important in themselves, are remembered, but cannot be confidently placed in a correct sequence—the raid on St. Nazarre, the sinking of the Graf Spee and the Bismarck, the landing of Hess in Scotland. So it is only the main landmarks in the developing story that Mark places clearly in sequence. Particularly if Mark had worked with Peter, some of the main landmarks and their relation to each other would have been remembered, even if the context of individual episodes could no longer be identified. Both C. H. Dodd and Vincent Taylor found themselves convinced of the authenticity of the basic outline into which Mark builds his narrative.

This outline is as follows:

(1) Jesus came from Nazareth in Galilee.

(2) He was baptized by John the Baptist, and this proved a moment of deep significance for him.

(3) He started his public ministry somewhat later.

(4) He called disciples to follow him.

(5) He became known for his message about God's rule as something very near and very real, and also as a teacher of penetrating insight. He used the novel method of parables to press home the truths about God's rule and to answer criticisms laid against him personally.

(6) He had great powers to heal the sick and disabled, provided he could awaken "faith" in the patient.

(7) He selected twelve from a larger number of his disciples for a more intimate association with himself, and for a full-time commitment to his ministry.

(8) Later he sent them out on missions to cover a wider area than he himself could reach.

(9) A moment of new understanding of the significance of Jesus came to some of the disciples at Caesarea Philippi.

(10) The antagonism of the religious leaders to Jesus, which had shown itself early in his ministry, began to assume more threatening proportions.

(11) In spite of the obvious danger Jesus defiantly left Galilee for Jerusalem in order to be there at the time of the annual Passover festival.

(12) He observed a last supper with his closest friends.

(13) As a result of assistance from one of the disciples, Judas, Jesus was arrested quietly at night by the Jewish authorities (perhaps with Roman assistance) and condemned by Jewish law as a blasphemer and heretic. He was then represented to the Roman authorities as a threat to the Roman peace, probably because some zealots wanted to find in him a political Messiah. So he was executed by crucifixion.

(14) His death, however, did not prove to be the end of it all.

There are other items that one or another may wish to add, as for instance the withdrawal of Jesus and his disciples, after the mission of the disciples, to an area north of Galilee. But the basic pattern as outlined above, drawn from Mark's narrative, can, I believe, be accepted as basically historical.

Degrees of Certainty

We have seen that there are features of the person, life, and bearing of Jesus and also a developing outline of the main events in his ministry that can be accepted as authentic. There are also other items that we have had to characterize as inauthentic—such as the later modifications that Matthew and Luke imposed on the earlier narrative of Mark, and stories that in themselves sound improbable and out of character with what we know of Jesus and which occur in only one single source, particularly if that one source is M (e.g., the coin in the fish's mouth, Peter walking on the water, etc.). Sayings and incidents that seem to reflect the situation of the early Church rather than the actual time of Jesus also have to be placed in this category, for example, the closing words of Matthew's gospel and, probably, the two references to the "Church" in Matthew, etc.

In between the certainties and the improbabilities there lie many incidents and sayings that we should have to categorize as "possible" but uncertain. They lack the sure note of authenticity, and yet have an element of probability in them. In many of these cases there may be an authentic nucleus that has been amplified by inauthentic material. These items cannot be classified with confidence. Some would describe them as basically authentic, others as largely inauthentic.

In this indeterminate category we may well have to place such items as the following, to name a few instances out of many:

(1) The confession of Jesus as the Christ at Caesarea Philippi. Mark in his gospel makes this the great dividing line in the ministry of Jesus, and almost certainly it represents a decisive moment in the ministry of Jesus. Even allowing that as the story was told and retold it might have changed its shape and content a little, the form in which Mark records it in Mark 8:27-30 has a strong claim to authenticity. Jesus and his disciples have left Galilean territory and are to the north of Gentile territory. If this story was an invention it is very hard to see why such an unexpected geographical location should be chosen for it. As they walk along Jesus asks his disciples what people are saying about him and how they assess him. They tell him that some identify him with John the Baptist, some with Elijah, others with some other Old Testament prophet. Then he asks what they themselves are thinking and Peter answers: "Thou art the Christ."

Bultmann approaches this material in his *History of the Synoptic Tradition* (p. 257) with the utmost skepticism. He writes about it: "This passage is to be characterized as legend. In no sense does the naming of the place in v. 27 ensure the historical character of what is told. . . . 'In the way' is a typical Markan comment, serving to introduce the piece of traditional material into his design (cp. 10:17, 32; 9:33 f.). . . . The fact that Jesus takes the initiative with his question itself suggests that this narrative is secondary, . . . as does the content of the question altogether. Why does Jesus ask about something on which he is bound to be every bit as well informed as were the

disciples? The question is intended simply to provoke the
answer; in other words it is a literary device. Once more
the disciples appear here as a medium between Jesus and
the people . . . , i.e., the disciples represent the Church,
and the passage gives expression to the specific judge-
ment which the Church had about Jesus, in distinction
from that of those outside. This then is a legend of faith:
faith in the Messiahship of Jesus is traced back to a story
of the first Messianic confession which Peter made about
Jesus." Others who take a similar point of view describe
it as "dramatized dogma" rather than an actual incident.

We note that Bultmann's statement consists of affirmations rather than convincing arguments. To many people
the mention of the area where this incident took place,
especially as it seems such an unlikely place to have been
invented for this particular purpose, sounds probable and
gives the episode a feeling of reliability. The fact that
Mark locates two or three episodes in his gospel (not very
many) as happening "in the way," that is, as Jesus and
his disciples move from place to place, is quoted as evidence of a fabrication. It could, however, quite as well
be true that these references represent actual memories.
The fact that Jesus raises the question rather than someone else is taken as a sign of inauthenticity. Only that
is authentic which begins from someone else. This seems
a very arbitrary judgment. In his teaching Jesus frequently
assumes the initiative by putting questions, trying to draw
the right answer from the other person. Is it therefore
so unusual for Jesus to put the question here? Bultmann
further sees it as obviously artificial that Jesus should
need to ask what people are saying about him since "he
is bound to be as well informed as the disciples." This
seems curiously incorrect. Who knows more about what
people think of a minister in a church, the minister
himself or his deacons? It would seem to be quite obvious that people would speak more freely about Jesus
in the presence of his disciples than in the actual presence of Jesus himself.

Personally I find Bultmann's affirmation at this point

quite unconvincing, and would think it much more probable that the incident is based on an actual event, even
though legendary additions may have attached themselves
to the original nucleus.

(2) There are some accounts of experiences of Jesus
that are often written off as the invention of the later
Church, produced for the purposes of its own teaching.
Included among these are the experience of Jesus at the
time of his baptism by John and the story of the tempta-
tion of Jesus as told in Matthew and Luke.

In Mark the experience of Jesus at the time of the baptism is entirely personal to himself. It is not a public
event in which others share. Either therefore the report
of what he heard God saying to him and what he experienced comes from Jesus himself, as he at some later
time told his disciples what the baptism had meant to
him, or else it is all Church invention. It seems to me
personally that what the occasion of the baptism meant
to Jesus is the kind of thing that Jesus would in fact
want to talk to his disciples about at some appropriate
later time. The visual symbolism of the heavens being
"opened" and the Spirit "like a dove" appear to me in
character with the pictorial method of the teaching of
Jesus as we know it elsewhere.

The story of the temptations has widely been relegated to the realm of the fable; but this also is something
that Jesus could well have talked about to his disciples
in the course of their later instruction. Once again the
vivid pictorial symbolism corresponds more closely to
what we know of Jesus' methods of teaching than to
those employed, so far as we know, in the early Church.
Moreover, the apparent meaning of the temptations ac-
cords more with the emphases we find elsewhere in the
life and ministry of Jesus than with the expectations of
the early Church.

(3) Mark records three predictions of the passion, when
Jesus speaks in anticipation of his coming suffering and
death. We have already noted that the third of these
(Mark 10:33) has been adjusted to tally more exactly with

the actual later events of the passion and death of Jesus, and we recognize that these adjustments are later additions by the Church. But does not this very fact suggest that the earlier predictions (Mark 8:31; 9:31), which are less precisely similar to the later events, have some basic historical authenticity behind them? They have, however, been commonly regarded as constructions of the early Church, as it sought to ascribe to Jesus an accurate foreknowledge of what lay ahead of him.

Foreknowledge, in general terms, is not, however, at all improbable. Martin Luther King, as he found himself the accepted leader of the civil rights movement, soon sensed that the work he had taken up was fraught with the darkest dangers. He spoke to his wife of the violent end that he had begun to see was inevitable in the circumstances of the time, and deliberately made his decision to maintain the course he had chosen in full knowledge of the cost he would have to pay. If Dr. King could speak calmly and clearly about a doom that he felt hung over him—as in fact it did—is it at all improbable that Jesus had some clear anticipation of the course of coming events, as they were likely to affect him?

To me it would seem most probable that as official hostility hardened against him Jesus would see that suffering and death lay ahead, but believed that ultimate triumph for his cause could be looked for beyond his death. It is, of course, quite probable that the precise form of his "predictions" would come to be influenced by the way later events actually worked out.

(4) The question is asked: Did Jesus know himself to be the Christ, as later Christians came to acknowledge him? In Mark's account he does not make any acknowledgment of it, until he is before the high priest at his trial. Some forms of the text even at this point (Mark 14:62) make the reply of Jesus not so much an acknowledgment as an indication that he is aware that some people are speaking of him in this way. The other gospels are less restrained than Mark, which is another reason for thinking that Mark's guarded reporting of the

issue is near the truth of the matter. W. E. Bundy, in
Jesus and the First Three Gospels, who takes what is substantially the same point of view as Bultmann about historicity, writes (p. 295): "It seems inconceivable that a
man of sane mind and sound heart, such as Jesus certainly
was, could ever have regarded himself as the Messiah."
This seems an extreme statement, since other men believed themselves to be Messiah without being totally de-
ranged. The whole question, however, is badly phrased
when put in this way. It is not so much whether Jesus
thought of himself as *The* Messiah, as though this was
a perfectly clear and distinct category. It was very far
from being a cut-and-dried concept. People had widely
different ideas about it. The question is rather whether
Jesus was willing to understand the task that God had
assigned to him in terms of the current ideas about Messiahship.

To me personally it seems probable that he avoided it,
and that he preferred to work out his own way of ful-
filling his work for God rather than have himself squeezed
by popular expectation into a category that seriously
distorted the nature of his task. It was quite different after
Jesus died. Then the nature of his mission had been made
clear for his disciples by his self-giving in death. Then
they could say: "This was the Messiah which God had
promised and which the Jewish people had been expect-
ing in a totally wrong way."

My own personal belief would be that Jesus knew that
he was entrusted by God with a task of unique significance. He called men to accept God's rule in their lives
and felt himself to be the bearer of this rule. He could
offer it to men and invite men to accept it. The desire on
the part of some to identify his role with that of the Jewish
Messiah did not commend itself to him, though it contained a degree of truth, since to call him Messiah was
for them the way of acknowledging him as God's messen-
ger in the highest degree conceivable. He was deeply
concerned to be totally obedient to God and to reflect
the Truth of God in all he said and did—as the Messiah

should. But one doubts whether he ever suggested to others that he should be thought of as Messiah. It was a category that needed a totally new interpretation before it adequately represented what he had come to do.

(5) Another name that is used of Jesus commonly in the gospels is that of Son of Man. Some recent scholars have argued that this, too, comes from the Church rather than from Jesus. It was one way in which the early Church expressed its estimation of the greatness of Jesus. One fact in particular tells strongly against this: it is the curious consistency with which the gospels always place this name only on the lips of Jesus himself. No one but Jesus uses it. It seems strange that this consistency would be imposed onto the material if it was a title invented for Jesus by the early Church. In that case other people rather than Jesus—or at any rate, as well as Jesus—would have been the ones to ascribe it to him.

If one ventures a personal opinion, it is that Jesus did speak of the "Son of Man" and in some cases at least referred to himself by it. Some of the Son of Man sayings in the gospels, however, may have been added later by the Church. Christian people, knowing that Jesus had spoken in this way of himself, introduced the phrase "Son of Man" into sayings ascribed to Jesus, where originally it had not occurred.

(6) The Transfiguration is another event that Bultmann and others would ascribe entirely to the work of the early Church. Bultmann writes of it (*History of the Synoptic Tradition,* p. 259): "It has long since been recognized that this legend was originally a resurrection story.... The Mountain to which Jesus leads the disciples is basically the same as the mountain in Mt. 28:16, that is, the mountain where the disciples met Jesus by appointment after the resurrection." Bultmann denies that the phrase "six days later" (Mark 9:2) is historical, and argues that such dating is found elsewhere only in the passion narrative. "In any event," he writes, "the sixth day is traditionally the day of Epiphany." It is not clear what this last statement is meant to prove. The story, we read, was intro-

duced by Mark "to serve as a heavenly ratification of Peter's confession and as a prophecy of the Resurrection in pictorial form."

There are features of the story, however, that to others have the appearance of historicity. These are the precise dating: "after six days" (probably in relation to Peter's confession); Peter's reference to Jesus as "Rabbi" (the Aramaic or Hebrew title, rather than the Greek "Lord"); Peter's suggestion about the erection of tents for spiritual visitors—a suggestion so ridiculous that Mark comments: "He didn't know what to say; for they were extremely frightened." Neither the fatuous words of Peter nor the excuse that he was just talking without first thinking are quite what one would expect the early Church to invent concerning its first apostle.

It is probably impossible now to reach with any degree of certainty the actual historical nucleus behind the story as we have it. Its constant use in the teaching work of the Church could well have led to some changes in it. It is possible also that Jesus himself spoke to his disciples about the strange experience after it had happened and that some of his explanations came to be incorporated in the story itself. But the historical features just named make it very probable that we have here what basically is a factual event, in which the disciples were brought into a new sense of the significance of Jesus, especially in his relation to God.

(7) Some people feel most strongly that the accounts of the resurrection of Jesus should surely come into the category of absolute historical certainty. If by that we mean that the disciples became absolutely certain that the death of Jesus was not the end of him, and that his activity among them continued to be real and effective, then that is one of the certainties. It is when we go further and ask what form the appearance of the risen Jesus took, physical or spiritual, that we cannot produce evidence from the gospels that provides a certain answer. Sometimes his presence appears to be physical, as when he takes food with his disciples; sometimes it is not physical, as when

he appears before them in spite of locked doors. More-over, what happened at the tomb is not clear. The evan-gelists tell the story of how it was found to be empty in different, even inconsistent ways. There is, however, una-nimity that the tomb was empty, though how or why we are not precisely told. One has to agree that once the continuity of the activity of Jesus was accepted as sure beyond any doubt, the attempt to explain it might well include the conviction that the tomb must have been empty. What, however, has an unmistakable note of his-toricity about it is that the people who discovered the tomb to be empty were women. At that time, in that part of the world, a woman's evidence was not regarded as valid, and it is therefore incredible that anyone who wanted to provide fabricated support for a doubtful story would put forward the idea that the tomb had been found empty by a woman. A fabricator would have fabricated some more reliably convincing evidence than that.

Historically we have to be content to leave the matter there—that the women who went to the tomb on Sunday morning found it empty and that the disciples as a whole became absolutely sure of the reality of the continuing activity of Jesus among them.

These seven items merely serve to illustrate what we mean by the category of items that are "possible" but "uncertain" in their historicity. Is there any way of reach-ing a more definite conclusion about the degree of his-torical fact they contain? At the moment we must be con-tent to leave them in the category of "not proven." Any decision we take will probably have a large element of subjective impression in it. It is, however, in this area of uncertainty that the argument of "consistency" can be introduced. Where some item is "possible," it may be upgraded into the category of "probable" if it can be shown to be wholly consistent with the other material assigned on rational grounds to the area of historical fact.

Chapter 9

The Teaching of Jesus

We now have to ask how far the teaching material ascribed to Jesus in the synoptic gospels may be regarded as authentic. There may well be historical material from the teaching of Jesus in the fourth gospel, but this is less immediately evident than in the synoptic gospels. In fact, the difference in style in this area, if nothing else, gives the synoptic gospels by comparison an air of authenticity. It is with the synoptic gospels that we are primarily concerned.

Even the most extreme Form Critics, who think that in the period of oral transmission the faith of the early Church transformed beyond recognition the actual historical events, agree that the teaching materials are much less likely to have suffered serious distortion than the narratives. Even then, it would be asserted, the teaching was by no means left unaffected.

The grounds we have already given for believing generally in the presence of reliable material in the synoptic gospels also support an assumption that in them there will be historical material on the recorded teaching of Jesus. But there are additional and more precise reasons that can be put forward as well.

For instance, two Scandinavian scholars, Riesenfeld and Gerhardsson, have made important contributions at this point. They start from the fact that Jesus was a teacher and was recognized as a teacher by his contemporaries. It appears that he was even called "Rabbi," a semi-official title for a teacher among the Jews. They argue from this that Jesus probably used some of the conventional methods customary among Rabbis in their teaching. They have shown that at that time the Rabbis believed dogmatically in the necessity of their disciples memorizing the subject matter to be studied. Pupils had to learn by heart the passage for study before the explanation of its meaning was given. Long sections of the Old Testament had to be memorized word for word. If this was so in Rabbinic schools, these scholars argue, then Jesus almost certainly used something of the same method, and required his disciples to learn by heart the material he taught, so that they in turn could teach it verbatim to others. In this case one would confidently expect that much of the teaching of Jesus would be preserved with great accuracy, since a group of disciples had learned to repeat it word for word. It is suggested that the reason why, when the contents of the canon of the New Testament were being fixed, the question of the apostolic authorship of a document counted for so much, was that it was known that the essential core of the teaching of Jesus had been committed to them, and they were the ones who could reproduce it faithfully.

Not everyone is persuaded by the arguments of these two scholars, but there may well be some weight in them. So far from the teaching of Jesus being left drifting on the air at the mercy of any careless or prejudiced reporter, it may be that some of it at any rate was taught in such a way as to enable it to be remembered and preserved faithfully.

There is, of course, doubt about the authenticity of some of the individual sayings ascribed to Jesus, but the teaching as a whole is so inwardly consistent in style as well as in content, so marked by an inner coherence,

that it is incredible that it could come from some amalgam
of sources and not from some single mind of great originality and distinctiveness. Throughout the recorded teaching of Jesus there are recurring features of style that can
be accounted for much more convincingly by ascribing
them to one single mind than to an anonymous community
consisting of widely different types of people.

Some of these characteristics—almost idiosyncrasies—are
as follows:

(1) Many of the sayings of Jesus fall into a rhythmic
pattern very similar to that of Hebrew poetry. This relied
on balance of thought and parallelism of word and phrase
rather than on strict meter and rhyme. Many of the sayings of Jesus are cast in just this kind of pattern, which
we find also in the psalms and the so-called poetical sections of the prophetic writings. The parallelism can be
of different kinds:

For instance, there is synonymous parallelism where the
same thought is expressed in two different ways:

> Are you able to drink the cup that I drink,
> > or to be baptized with the baptism with which
> > I am baptized? (Mark 10:38).
> Ask and it will be given you;
> Seek and you will find,
> > Knock, and it will be opened to you (Matt. 7:7).

Sometimes the parallelism expresses a contrast, and is
then known as antithetic parallelism:

> Whoever would save his life will lose it,
> Whoever loses his life . . . will save it (Mark 8:35).

Or it may be an advancing parallelism, in which the second part repeats something from the first part and develops
it:

> Whoever receives one such child . . . receives me,
> Whoever receives me, receives . . . him who sent me
> > (Mark 9:37).

These are instances of the different types of parallelism
that constantly recur in the recorded words of Jesus in
the synoptic gospels. It is a characteristic feature of his

teaching style. One can well believe that this was the
way Jesus actually spoke on certain occasions. It is hardly
conceivable that "community creations" would produce
such a mannerism consistently. If some were produced
on this pattern it could only be because an unmistakable
pattern had already been provided that they felt compelled
to try to imitate. The original pattern must have come
from Jesus himself.

(2) Another feature of the teaching material in the
synoptic gospels is that if it is translated back into the
original Aramaic (as has been done by such scholars as
Matthew Black and J. Jeremias) one finds instances of
assonance and alliteration, not apparent in the Greek
of the New Testament, but wholly in tune with the style
of proverbial parallelism. This again is a feature not likely
to be reproduced in community creations—particularly in
communities whose native tongue was not Aramaic.

(3) A third characteristic of the teaching material of
Jesus is the way in which Jesus is constantly asking questions in order to get the person addressed to give his
mind to the subject and reach his own decision. Only a
few typical instances out of very many need be given: "If
you love those who love you, what credit is that to you?"
(Luke 6:32 = Q); "Can a blind man lead a blind man?"
(Luke 6:39 = Q); "Why do you see the speck in your
brother's eye, but do not notice the log in your own eye?"
(Luke 6:41 = Q); "What did you go out into the wilder-
ness to behold? A reed shaken by the wind?... A man
clothed in soft raiment?... A prophet?" (Luke 7:24-26 =
Q); "To what shall we compare the men of this generation?" (Luke 7:31 = Q); "What father among you, if his
son asks for a fish, will instead of a fish give him a serpent?" (Luke 11:11 = Q); "Does he not leave the ninety-
nine in the hills and go in search of the one that went
astray?" (Matt. 18:12 = M); "Did you not agree with me
for a denarius?... Am I not allowed to do what I choose
with what belongs to me? Or do you begrudge me my
generosity?" (Matt. 20:13-15 = M); "Which of them will
love him more?" (Luke 7:42 = L); "Which of these three

proved neighbor?" (Luke 10:36 = L). Similarly, this characteristic question-style is found in Mark (e.g., at 2:9, 19; 8:36-37, etc.).

Clearly this method of putting a question to elicit from the other person his own answer is a consistent feature of the type of teaching ascribed to Jesus. The only possible explanation of it seems to be that it was in fact a mannerism of Jesus that his reporters faithfully recorded. If imitations of it came from the early Church this is only because they had a well-established pattern that they accepted as their guide.

(4) A fourth curious mannerism in the teaching of Jesus is his fondness for a threefold form of expression. There is, of course, nothing peculiar in this itself. Threefoldness seems part of a proverbial way of speaking that everybody uses to some extent. We speak of "every Tom, Dick, and Harry." Caesar used the aphorism: "I came, I saw, I conquered." What is peculiar in the gospels, however, is the extraordinary frequency with which Jesus chose to speak in this threefold way. It can be instanced from almost every page of the synoptic gospels. By quite startling contrast it is almost totally absent from the fourth gospel. The only threefold expression there placed on the lips of Jesus is: "I am the Way, the Truth, and the Life." In John, however, we are dealing largely with teaching that is the product of Christian faith and community. It is in John that we have good evidence of the manner in which the early Church placed its ideas on the lips of Jesus, and there we have no recurrent threefoldness. The fact that this threefoldness pervades all the synoptic teaching tradition and is absent from the fourth gospel has its readiest explanation in the assumption that what the synoptics give us in this respect is an authentic account of the teaching of Jesus himself.

Further assurance that this mannerism goes right back to Jesus himself comes from the fact that it appears in all four of the primary sources. A quick count gives sixty-four instances altogether (counting parallels or triplicates in different gospels as only one). Of these, nineteen may be assigned to Q, seventeen to L, fourteen to Mark, and nine to M. Five remaining cannot be confidently assigned to any one of the primary sources. A few typical instances may be given. Anxious human beings ask: "What shall we eat? or What shall we drink? or Wherewithal shall we be clothed?" (Matt. 6:31 = Luke 12:29 = Q). "Thou gavest me no water for my feet, . . . no kiss, . . . my head with oil thou didst not anoint" (Luke 7:45 = L). "If thy hand, . . . foot, . . . or eye offend thee, . . ." (Mark 9:43). There are three types of "eunuch": those born so, those made eunuchs by men, and those who make themselves eunuchs for the sake of the Kingdom of God (Matt. 19:12 = M).

The fact that all four primary sources reflect this mannerism independently means that it certainly goes back to Jesus himself. This feature of threefoldness may indeed sometimes help us to distinguish a genuine word of Jesus from one that has been modified in the tradition. Where either Matthew or Luke (perhaps pressed for space) records a saying of Jesus in a twofold form and the other has it in a threefold form, there may be good reason for preferring the threefold version. Similarly, where Matthew and Luke each records a saying of Jesus in a twofold form but using three items in all between them, it probably means that an original threefold form of the saying was the one Jesus spoke. For instance, when a father's care for his child is being described, Matthew (7:10) says a father would not give the child a stone when asked for bread or a serpent for a fish; Luke (11:12) says he would not give him a serpent for a fish, or a scorpion for an egg. One imagines that the original saying of Jesus included all three items: bread and stone, fish and serpent, egg and scorpion.

But the main point is not so much that in some cases it enables us to determine which of two possibilities is nearer to the original word of Jesus. The very fact of threefoldness to this extent in the teaching of Jesus and the fact of its occurrence frequently in each of the primary sources makes it as sure as it can be that this is

an original characteristic of the teaching of Jesus. And
the fact that all four of these sources do retain this feature so clearly increases our confidence in their own
faithfulness to the teaching of Jesus at points where we
cannot precisely check it.[1]

(5) A fifth characteristic of the teaching of Jesus is the
way in which he used words from the common life of
the ordinary man to convey deep truths about God and
human life. He avoids all theological or philosophical
terms, but clothes his teaching in the ordinary words of
normal conversation, words for animals and birds, plants
and trees, and simple things from the world of nature and
the household and the farm. Here again words of this kind
are comparatively rare in the fourth gospel.

If this particular feature has not previously been pointed
out to us, it comes as a great surprise to discover how
many animals and plants are used by Jesus in his teaching.
The following does not claim to be a complete list, but
it is an impressive one: ass, calf, camel, chicken, cock,
dog, dove, eagle, fish, fox, gnat, hen, ox, pig, scorpion,
serpent, sheep, sparrow, wolf. From plant-life the following: lilies, grass, figs, thistles, weeds, wheat, plant, tree,
seed, fruit, harvest, branches. Common features from the
world of nature to appear are: salt, sun, rain, wind, rock,
sand, field, pit, leaven, dough. And manufactured articles
commonly used in the home, farm, or workshop include:
lamps, oven, gate, door, house, staff, coat, shoes, wallet,
barns, yoke, plank, dust, net, trumpet. This skill at using
homely objects to illuminate his teaching about spiritual
truths is the mark of an original mind, not of a miscellane-
ous community.

(6) The dominance of the Kingdom of God is also
without doubt a genuine characteristic of the actual teaching of Jesus. The phrase did occur in the Old Testament,
but not commonly. In contemporary Judaism the phrase
was known, but it was not generally used. In any case

---

[1] For a fuller treatment of this particular phenomenon see "Threefoldness in the Teaching of Jesus" by C. L. Mitton in The Expository
Times, LXXV, 228.

the way Jesus spoke about the Kingdom of God as now
breaking in upon men and not just as belonging to the
end of the ages in some remote future, was different from
anything in contemporary use. Moreover, it cannot have
been imposed on the gospels by the custom of the early
Church, because the phrase "Kingdom of God" quickly
dropped out of general use after the death of Jesus. Paul
uses it occasionally, but only as a phrase that belongs to
the tradition from the past, not as one of his own choice.
In the fourth gospel the phrase occurs only twice. Elsewhere in the New Testament, apart from some references
in Revelation, it is even rarer than in Paul's writings. Yet
the phrase dominates the words of Jesus in the synoptic
tradition. Mark tells us that his message was centered on
it. "The Kingdom of God is at hand" is Mark's summary
of the proclamation of Jesus. Many of the recorded sayings of Jesus have to do with "entering" or "receiving"
the Kingdom. Many of his parables are specifically related to the Kingdom.

This way of speaking of the Kingdom is not characteristic of Judaism or the early Church. It must be something original to Jesus.

Further supporting evidence for this conclusion is that
the prominence of the Kingdom of God in the teaching
of Jesus is found in all four primary sources.

(7) Reference has already been made to individual features of the teaching of Jesus that must come from him
and not from the later influence of the Church. Among
these are included the use of "Abba" as the name by which
he addressed God in prayer, and the unusual way in which
he used the word "Amen," not to confirm what had already been said but to introduce some emphatic affirmation—a peculiar usage not known either in contemporary
Judaism or the early Church.

There is no evidence that "Abba" was ever used to
address God in Jewish circles, and, as we saw earlier, its
later use by Greek Christians can only have come from
the tradition that Jesus himself had used it. Mark records
Jesus as using "Abba" in the garden of Gethsemane (Mark

14:36), and it is more than likely that it was this particular word which was used on other occasions when the gospels simply translate as "Father"—as, for instance, in the opening of the Lord's Prayer. So the use of "Abba" and "Amen" may be accepted as an authentic part of the teaching of Jesus.

(8) Within the teaching material in the gospels there is no area where we may legitimately feel ourselves so near to the actual words of Jesus as in the parables. Jeremias speaks of them as "a fragment of the original rock of tradition." In them he believes that we hear "the authentic voice of Jesus" ("*ipsissima vox Jesu*").

Unhappily the traditional way of interpreting the parables had largely obscured their original significance. This was, first, because it treated the parables as disembodied stories portraying eternal truths, and, second, it invested the details of the stories with subtle allegorical significance, which could not conceivably have been understood by the first hearers, even if it were edifying to Christians of later generations. By this device the two pence and the inn in the parable of the Good Samaritan could be expounded as representing the later sacraments of the Church and the Church itself—something totally foreign to anything in the original intention of the parable.

It is chiefly to J. Jeremias and C. H. Dodd that this generation owes a new understanding of the parables of Jesus. Dodd in his book *The Parables of the Kingdom* and Jeremias, building on Dodd's insights in his book *The Parables of Jesus,* both insisted that the parables can only be understood in their original significance if we realize that they were addressed to actual and particular occasions in the ministry of Jesus. They also followed further the lead given earlier by Jülicher and demonstrated the falsity of the allegorical interpretations that had become traditional in the Church. It was now shown that the purpose of a parable lay in its one main thrust, not in its many details. And its meaning lay in its applicability to something in the actual context of the ministry of Jesus. That is, each parable arose out of an actual historical situation.

The original meaning of a parable is sometimes obscured by the gospel writers themselves. They, like subsequent exponents, were concerned not with the original meaning of each parable but with the application of it to the needs of the people of their own time. To make it relevant to their own time they sometimes changed items in the parable itself, but more often it was by the context in which they placed the parable or by the other sayings of Jesus that they attached to it that they indicated how they themselves or the Church of their own day felt the parable ought to be understood and applied to current issues.

Some parables, for instance, when Jesus first spoke them, were intended to alert his listeners to the crisis that faced them in his own ministry. God was confronting them in the person and message of Jesus with the need to make a positive response immediately. A generation later these parables calling for urgent decision were applied to the different crisis that Christians of that time felt was confronting them—that is, the imminence of the Second Coming of Christ. The parables of the Ten Virgins and the Thief in the Night probably belong to this group. Sometimes also parables that originally were defiant challenges to the critics and opponents of Jesus were adjusted in the later teaching of the Church to give them a message applicable to Christians of that later time. This probably happened to the parable of the Talents. An instance where further sayings of Jesus were added to a parable to suggest how it should be understood is found in the parable of the Unjust Steward (Luke 16:1-8) and the originally separate sayings about wealth that have been assembled and attached to it at the end (Luke 16:9-13). Sometimes two parables have been fused into one in order to support some current emphasis in the Church. This probably is true of the way Matthew has inserted the story about the missing wedding garment into the story of the Great Feast. There is also the tendency to heighten the effect by introducing exaggerations.

One of the great contributions of Jeremias' book on the parables is that he analyzes what these tendencies were in the Church at the end of the first century that in some degree distorted the original form of the parables (pp. 20-83 in the first edition). When we have been enabled to detect what are later embellishments, it becomes possible, by eliminating them, to discover the form of the story as Jesus first told it. In this way, Jeremias claims, we find ourselves in the presence of the very words of Jesus.

The parables, therefore, when stripped of later embellishments and misleading interpretations suggested by false contexts, are part of the original, historical teaching of Jesus. They are not the product of the later Christian community. On what grounds may we make this claim and hold it to be true?

(1) These parables of Jesus are something quite peculiar to Jesus himself. They do not belong to any familiar literary category already in use in contemporary Judaism. The Jewish background does not provide any real parallel to them, nor does later Christian literature. Jeremias' judgment (in his *New Testament Theology*, I, 29) is: "We find nothing to be compared with the parables of Jesus whether in the intertestamental literature of Judaism, the Essene writings, in Paul or in Rabbinic literature." In the Old Testament there were some "fables" (sometimes mistakenly called "parables") in which trees, plants, and animals behave like human beings and converse together. But there are no such fables in the teaching of Jesus. Plants and animals do not speak in his parables. "Jesus regularly uses the familiar metaphors mostly drawn from the Old Testament and familiar to everyone of that time," but he does not tell fables or allegories (so Jeremias). Instead "his parables take us into the midst of throbbing everyday life. Their nearness to life, their simplicity and clarity, the masterly brevity with which they are told, the seriousness of their appeal to conscience, their lov-

ing understanding of the outcasts of religion"—all this is
without parallel.

On the basis of our fourth criterion of genuineness, that
of "dissimilarity," the parables of Jesus have every mark
of being authentic.

(2) The parables fit exactly into what is known of the
geography, climate, and social conditions of Jewish Palestine at the time of Jesus. The Sower sets about his task
as a sower would in that area. The "Good Samaritan" reflects the notorious dangers of the journey between Jerusalem and Jericho. Local customs about weddings, banquets, family relationships, etc. are all accurately represented. It is in Palestine where Jesus lived and taught
that these conditions were found, not in Rome or Ephesus.
The accuracy of the parables in reflecting the conditions
of that time strongly suggest that they are historical to
the ministry of Jesus.

(3) The contents of the parables also are at home in
the historical situation of the ministry of Jesus. Some of
them directly reflect the conflicts in which Jesus was
involved with the Pharisees and scribes, and indeed are
part of his answer to their criticisms of him and his teaching and conduct. Jeremias has vividly described this class
of parables as "weapons of war." They provide, for instance, part of the answer of Jesus to his enemies' criticism of his disregard of their strict sabbath rules, when
the rigid observance of them would have hindered him
in helping someone in need. They give his answer also
to their protest about his free and easy association with
those who were right outside the official religious insti-
tutions of that time. This polemic purpose of the parables
is indeed recognized in the gospels themselves. Mark at
12:12 comments: "The Pharisees tried to arrest him, for
they perceived that he had told this parable against them."
So too at Luke 15:2 it is precisely noted that what stirred
Jesus to tell the three stories about the Lost Sheep, the
Lost Coin, and the Lost Son was the criticism that the
Pharisees directed against him because he sought the
company of "sinners" and even shared in their hospitality.

The nearest parallel in the Old Testament to the parabolic method of Jesus is the story told by Nathan the prophet to King David. The king had behaved very unscrupulously. He had committed adultery with the wife of one of his soldiers during the soldier's absence on military service. Nathan tells an apparently factual story about an act of gross injustice committed by one of David's subjects. A rich man had used his power to take from a poor man the only lamb he possessed, a pet lamb greatly treasured by his family. In angrily declaring the rich man worthy of death, David passed judgment on himself. Nathan's pointed conclusion was: "Thou art the man," and this brought home to David the pointed significance of what at first had seemed the story of a deplorable action, but quite unrelated to himself. So the parables of Jesus, though superficially just interesting stories of no particular relevance, did in fact invite the Pharisees to approve conduct in others that in essence was the same as the conduct they were vehemently condemning in Jesus, and to disapprove of conduct in others that was roughly parallel to their own. The elder brother in the parable of the Prodigal Son is a thinly veiled portrayal of the Pharisees and their attitude to the outcast whom Jesus sought to befriend. That is why this parable and others like it are well called "weapons of war."

The parables therefore can be seen to fit exactly into the known historical situation of the time of Jesus. Thus they provide a double attestation. The historical situation confirms the historicity of the parables, and the parables confirm the historical situation presented in the synoptic gospels. Each confirms the authenticity of the other.

(4) The other parables that do not fall into this category of "weapons of war" are found to coincide exactly with features of the teaching of Jesus as it occurs elsewhere, especially the teaching related to the Kingdom of God.

Jesus called upon men to recognize that God was confronting them through his own ministry and message. He summoned them to repent and commit their lives without delay in obedience to God (Mark 1:15, 19-20). Some responded; others pleaded for delay and time to think it over. Three such incidents are given in Luke 9:57-62: each person involved says in effect: "Lord, I will . . . , but. . . ." It is to occasions precisely similar to these that several parables are addressed, calling for immediate and decisive action instead of temporizing and delay. Such parables as the Ten Virgins and the Rich Fool fall into this group.

There are moments in the gospels when the disciples became discouraged because some who had started as disciples were beginning to drift away. This same disappointment at the lack of encouraging results is evident in the parable of the Sower, with its recognition that there is indeed much apparent waste of time and energy, but nevertheless a worthwhile harvest can be depended on.

The rich young ruler, one representative of many, turns away from Jesus because he asks too much. Some of the parables fit just such an occasion. They symbolize the truth that no matter how much is asked, the price paid is nothing compared with the joy of finding the Kingdom (e.g., the parables of the Pearl and the Treasure in the Field).

Many must have felt that Jesus was engaged in a wild goose chase. What could one village carpenter and a few fishermen do to change the world? But Jesus insists that there is no limit to what God may do even when he has to work with only the slenderest of human resources. The parables of the seed growing secretly and the mustard seed fit in here.

In the parables, therefore, we see something quite new and original to Jesus, something derivable from no other known source; we see also something that is totally in accord with the social life of Palestine as it was at the time of Jesus; we also find that their message entirely coincides with what Jesus in other ways represented in his teaching. For such reasons the parables may be accepted as a particularly authentic element in the teaching material of Jesus. As we listen to them it is the very voice of Jesus that we are enabled to hear.

We may therefore regard the teaching material of Jesus as recorded in the synoptic gospels as the most reliably historical feature in these gospels. It has suffered some embellishments, distortions, and additions in the course of transmission, but these can often be detected. Moreover, the context in which sayings and parables are sometimes placed suggests an interpretation that reflects the thought of the Church rather than the original meaning of Jesus. When, however, these facts are allowed for, there remains a very large proportion of the teaching of Jesus that can legitimately be regarded as his very own.

ADDENDUM

How the various tests for ascertaining the genuineness of sayings attributed to Jesus may be applied can be illustrated from two instances taken from recent books.

In his book *Commands of Christ* (Abingdon) Professor Paul S. Minear discusses the saying of Jesus recorded in Mark 10:25: "It is easier for a camel to go through the eye of a needle than for a rich man to enter the Kingdom of God." He concludes that it is a genuinely historical utterance of Jesus and on pages 106-109 gives six reasons in support of his judgment:

(1) "It illustrates the rule that the more difficult reading, whether the difficulty be stylistic or ethical, is likely to be the earliest" (that is, as compared with some similar word that by comparison reduces the stringency of the saying).

(2) "It is so difficult a saying that it created a problem for the church from that day to this" (cf. Mark 10:26).

(3) "It must have had pristine authority to be preserved; it is hard to imagine any early Christian creating it" (changes in the tradition normally tend to weaken the impact of sayings).

(4) "In context this saying of Jesus is entirely consistent with other sayings about wealth."

(5) "The imagery is drawn from Jewish tradition and would be entirely clear to the rural folk of Galilee."

(6) "In form the saying is a hyperbole such as Jesus frequently used."

The second instance is taken from *Mark: Evangelist and Theologian* by Professor Ralph P. Martin (Paternoster). On pages 165-166 he discusses the authenticity of the saying of Jesus in Mark 8:12-13: "Why does this generation seek a sign? Truly, I say to you, no sign shall be given to this generation." He believes that in it "we hear a true accent of *ipsissima vox Jesu*," and gives the following as his reasons:

(1) "Mark's version of this saying, which forbids absolutely the granting of a sign, stands at the furthest recoverable point of the tradition." That is, the modified forms of the saying in Matthew and Luke are clearly later attempts to soften its severity.

(2) The saying is "introduced by the authorizing formula: 'Truly, I say to you....'" This is "a form of statement which J. Jeremias has claimed to go back to Jesus himself." In the Greek the word "truly" is in fact "amen." This is not a Greek word at all but a Hebrew word transliterated into Greek letters.

(3) The Greek words translated "No sign shall be given" are also clearly a literal translation of a Hebrew or Aramaic idiom. Literally the Greek words are: "If a sign shall be given to this generation..." (the protasis of a conditional sentence, without any apodosis following). In Greek it is meaningless; but it can be shown to be a literal translation of a Hebrew formula for making an extremely strong negative asseveration: "A sign will certainly not be given." Mark's Greek "obviously reflects his faithfulness to a very unusual type of wording."

(4) The passive form of the verb "shall be given" suggests a periphrasis for the divine name such as occurs also in Matthew 7:7. It means: "God will not give." "We are drawn back to Jesus' attested way of expressing himself by this use of a reverential circumlocution."

In addition to these arguments of Professor Martin, we may note also the presence of the question, which we have seen is a trait characteristic of the teaching method of Jesus.

CONCLUSION

Our investigations have given us grounds for believing that within the gospels we can discern much reliably historical material. This enables us to gain important factual information about Jesus in three areas:

(1) It provides a valid portrait of Jesus himself, of the main qualities of his life and his characteristic attitudes, as those who had known him remembered them. These were summarized on pages 102ff.

(2) It reveals a credible sequence of the outstanding events in his life and ministry, an outline of which was given on pages 123f.

(3) It contains a considerable amount of reliable teaching material, which can confidently be ascribed to Jesus himself. This would include, for the most part, those sayings which give evidence of coming from an Aramaic original, those which fall into the pattern of Hebrew parallelism, those which propound spiritual truth by means of everyday words taken from the common life of ordinary people, and the parables in their original form. This can be discovered when later embellishments have been eliminated, as was so convincingly done by Jeremias in his book on the parables.

This total picture of Jesus as he was remembered, a picture that we can accept as basically historical without

having to allow credulity to usurp our better judgment,
has two most significant features:

(1) The first is that it is not in any marked degree different from the picture of Jesus as we are familiar with
it in the synoptic gospels. Indeed, if our picture of Jesus
is one that we have derived from the material in the three
primary sources within the gospels rather than from the
later theological adjustments that occur in the editorial
work of Matthew, Luke and John, it is strikingly similar.

(2) The second is that it is a picture of a human life
of such outstanding quality that it is able to sustain the
explanation of it that the followers of Jesus felt themselves bound to give, and which in turn gave rise to the
affirmations of the kerygma. They believed that in this
figure of Jesus God himself had confronted men in judgment and in hope, as at no other point in human history.
They tried to interpret their understanding of him in
whatever contemporary words and phrases seemed least
inadequate to convey the sense of awe, gratitude, and
expectancy that the memory of him, combined with the
awareness of his living presence with them, aroused in
their hearts and minds. So they spoke of him as Christ,
Lord, Son of God, Word of God.

This historical figure, as we have been able to discover him, has enabled us to sense something of the remarkable qualities and powers in him that brought men
to confess him in these ways, and to declare that in him
God had become real to them as never before, that in
him God had taken decisive action for the good of man,
and that man's understanding of God's purposes had been
forever enriched through the life and death of Jesus of
Nazareth.

SELECT BIBLIOGRAPHY

Althaus, P. *The So-called Kerygma and the Historical Jesus*, 1958 (Oliver and Boyd).

Bornkamm, G. *Jesus of Nazareth*, 1960 (Hodder and Stoughton).
What Can We Know About Jesus?, 1969 (St. Andrew's Press).

Bultmann, R. *History of the Synoptic Tradition*, Eng. Tr. 1963 (Blackwell).

Dodd, C. H. *Parables of the Kingdom*, 1935 (Nisbet).
The Founder of Christianity, 1971 (Collins).

Jeremias, J. *The Parables of Jesus*, 1954 (SCM).
The Proclamation of Jesus, New Testament Theology, Vol. 1, 1973 (SCM).

Käsemann, E. *Essays on New Testament Themes*, 1954 (SCM).

Kähler, M. *Der sogenannte historische Jesus und der geschichtliche biblische Christus*, 1892, Leipzig.

McArthur, H. K. *In Search of the Historical Jesus*, 1969 (Scribners).

Nineham, D. E. *St. Mark*, 1963 (Pelican Commentary).

Taylor, V. *The Gospel According to St. Mark*, 1952 (Macmillan).
The Life and Ministry of Jesus, 1954 (Macmillan).

Zahrnt, H. *The Historical Jesus*, 1963 (Collins).